Schools of Solidarity

Families and Catholic Social Teaching

Mary M. Doyle Roche

LITURGICAL PRESS
Collegeville, Minnesota

www.litpress.org

1	2	3	4	5	6	7	8	9

Library of Congress Cataloging-in-Publication Data

Roche, Mary M. Doyle.
    Schools of solidarity : families and Catholic social teaching / Mary M. Doyle Roche.
      pages cm
    Includes bibliographical references.
    ISBN 978-0-8146-4807-0 — ISBN 978-0-8146-4832-2 (ebook)
    1. Families—Religious aspects—Catholic Church.   2. Families—Religious life.   3. Christian sociology—Catholic Church.   I. Title.

BX2351.R625   2015
261.8'3585—dc23   2014047040

Contents

for Emma Rose and Declan

Acknowledgements

Writing a book about families while trying to "do the family thing" at the same time has been a challenge, a rewarding challenge to be sure, but a challenge nonetheless. I write about family life not because my family has become a perfect school of solidarity, but because I see how much I have to learn about the many experiences that families have in striving to live out the gospel together. I write because I hope that the practice of writing as a form of "contemplation in action" will make me more attentive to the needs of my own family and of families who are both neighbor and stranger to me. I am thankful for the many ways that the members of my family, especially Emma Rose and Declan, pitched in so that I could take the needed time and space to write and for the love that sustains our life together.

I am grateful to Barry Hudock for the invitation to embark on this project with Liturgical Press, his continued guidance, and for modeling the kind of writing that is both accessible and engaging for interested readers. I am fortunate to have many colleagues in the field of Christian ethics who wrestle with the moral issues facing families as well as the implications of Catholic social teaching for the church today—many of them, though not all, are listed in the "For Further Study" section at the end of the book. This modest contribution to the conversation would not be possible without their insights. Thanks also to Andrew Edwards at Liturgical Press for managing the editorial process and bringing the project to fruition.

Introduction
The Classroom of Everyday Life

It is a typical evening in our home in a central Massachusetts suburb. My husband and I are sitting down to review "the calendar" or, perhaps more accurately, try to reconcile the many calendars stored in old-fashioned datebooks, looming large on the kitchen wall, covered with souvenir magnets on the refrigerator, and floating in "the cloud" to be drawn down to earth by the apps on our phones. We have both survived a day at work—he as an information technology professional for a nearby school district (thank heavens, or else I would be lying on my back in the yard, gazing up at clouds looking for my schedule!) and I as a professor of religious studies at a nearby Jesuit college. The dinner has been prepared and eaten, though lingering doubts fill my mind about where the food came from and whether anyone actually ate any of the vegetables. Some dishes have made it to the dishwasher in a happy moment in which everyone pitched in to help, but a Leaning Tower of Pisa of Pots (to which others in my family seem to be allergic) awaits me; they need to soak after all. Our two children persevered through their day in junior high and high school and after-school activities and have reluctantly set about their homework assignments; calls of "I need help" will punctuate the calendar conversation.

We are tired and pulled in many different directions, feeling stretched to the breaking point. What sounds catchy in our parish bulletin, "Time, Talent, and Treasure," we experience as overwhelming in practice. Who will do the drop-off at (two different) schools in the morning? Who will do the pick-up after school? Basketball practice? Art class? Who has to work late and when? There is a conflict with the kids' dental appointments. Is there a weekend available to visit grandparents in New York? How will one of us juggle things while the other is traveling for work? It is our turn to help with the delivery of meals to homeless families in our parish. Someone needs to get to the grocery store (a list to be made) and to the craft store for supplies for the science fair or the medieval castle project (another list). The car needs to be dropped off at the mechanic's on Saturday because we can't live without it during the week. Mounds of laundry are reaching Mt. Everest proportions and the dust bunnies look more like Irish wolfhounds. Date night? We laugh . . . or cry. The calendar conversation is draining; the budget conversation is even worse.

"The ordinary acts we practice every day at home are of more importance to the soul than their simplicity might suggest."

—*Thomas Moore, 19th c. Irish poet*

Though every family is unique, I imagine that our experience of being and becoming a family together is not unlike the experiences of many other families. And we are lucky. We enjoy relatively good health. We worry about finances and plans for the future but earn a good living at jobs we enjoy and have important benefits like health insurance and vacation time. Our children attend good schools and play in a relatively safe neighborhood. We have not yet reached the point where we are "sandwiched," responsible for growing children (or grandchildren) and aging, infirmed parents. We receive tremendous support from our extended family and friends. We have a traditional marriage and look like a tradi-tional family, so we enjoy all the social and economic privileges that such arrangements afford. We have time, talent, and treasure even though we are often a bit muddled when it comes to figuring out the best way to allocate those resources for the well-being of our family, friends, colleagues, community, students, parish, and those in need, some of whom we encounter in our daily lives and the billions of whom we will never meet. We strive to love God, ourselves, our neighbors, strangers, and even our enemies <u>but feel ourselves coming up short.</u>

This is who and where we are as a family. This is the context in which my family and many other families strive to live out the gospel. There are many more who strive to support their families, contribute to their communities, and live out their faith without many of the resources we have. Many families live in the context of material poverty, insecurity, and violence in their communities or political instability in their countries. We bring valuable gifts and talents to family life, but we bring limitations too. What may seem like a clear advantage at first, like economic security, may in fact blind us to the needs of our neighbor families struggling in poverty. Our vulnerabilities, which may appear as conditions we want to overcome, might also allow us to understand more deeply the suffering of others. It is in the context of everyday life that families encounter their strengths, their weaknesses, their sinfulness, and most importantly God's grace and the companionship of Jesus. Everyday life, the classroom of lived experience, is the place where families work out what it means to be and become a family together.

What Families Are Called to Do

The temptation faced by many families who have enough, perhaps even more than enough, is to shore things up, to maximize our security and comfort. We try to make sure that our children have everything they need and desire, to the point of trying to gain advantage over other people's children (going to the *right* schools, engaging in the *right* activities, etc.). There are voices within Christianity who would have our homes become fortresses, suggesting they are places to be walled off, fitted with battlements, or set in opposition to other families and the culture at large. Others think about families as "havens in a heartless world" where members (particularly fathers) enjoy a retreat from the messy and competitive world of work and politics. It can be a rather romantic view in which relationships in the home bear the sole responsibility for the emotional gratification of family members, a particularly heavy burden for spouses and children.

Whether considered a fortress or a haven, the <u>family is vulnerable to becoming an isolated unit</u>, turned in on itself. Though there is plenty of material in the traditions of the Catholic Church to bolster these views, there is another picture of the role of the family that emerges as the church has sought to engage the modern world and also reach back with new insight into the message of the gospel. This view is most pronounced in the traditions of Catholicism developed throughout the twentieth century and into the twenty-first. The emphasis is not on a family turned in on itself, but rather on a family turned outward toward others.

In words attributed to Antoine de Saint-Exupery (author of the classic *The Little Prince*), "Life has taught us love does not consist in gazing at each other, but in looking outward together in the same direction." Families strengthened by love look outward onto the world. But families who have their lives rooted in the gospel message of Jesus are not just looking anywhere at anything; they have their sights set on a particular vision. Theologian Tim Muldoon and his wife Sue Muldoon have insightfully called upon families to look at themselves and out into the world with "kingdom eyes." Jesus was proclaiming the kingdom of God, a kingdom in which the usual order of things would be turned upside down, in which many of the values of the day (and of our day too) would be challenged. Even the family itself would be challenged in light of a new family of faith in Christ, united not by blood but by the waters of baptism and the eucharistic meal.

The proclamation of the kingdom by Jesus Christ in the first century and the call to a new evangelization by Pope Francis in the twenty-first place the family in a complex relationship with the wider culture. There are important ways in which Christian families are called to be countercultural and to resist the influences of harmful trends in our society toward individualism, consumerism, and violence. They resist cultural messages about what it means to have achieved success, but resistance alone may not be enough. While they resist what passes for success in our society (wealth, status, advantage, influence), they also offer a different vision of success by how they live their lives. So, there are also important ways in which families participate in and seek to transform the society around them by engaging in service, work, worship, politics, art, the sciences, and so forth, with a view to a life well lived that is just, compassionate, and being willing to stand with those who are suffering.

Within Catholicism, the family has been variously referred to as the first "cell" of civil society, a domestic church, a school of humanity, a school of love, and a school of solidarity. Think of the cells of a living organism that function together for the life of the organism. Cells have boundaries but they also interact with other cells and the environment. Families are the most basic building blocks of society, the smallest and most intimate units in our communities. People, when the conditions are right, come to society through the family. Children are introduced to the world around them by their parents and other family members. Families are part of ever-widening and often-overlapping circles of relationship: building neighborhoods, schools, workplaces, governments, and parishes, and so forth. Indeed, Catholics might think of their parishes as "families of families."

There are many toy purchases that my husband and I have regretted, but we have never thought twice about the old-fashioned, simple (and expensive . . . it costs money to be simple!), wooden building blocks that arrived under the tree one Christmas and were added to in subsequent years. Our family has built many different structures with these blocks. When the children were little, the fun of course was in knocking them down within seconds of having erected them. But over time, the buildings became more complex: houses, castles, and even fortresses. The most wonderful part was that we could use our imaginations to build anything. We worked with some ideas about what a castle should have to make it recognizable as a castle (turrets, a mote, and bridge) but within those basic guidelines we could build something unique. Like a sonnet or a haiku, poems that must obey certain rules, within those boundaries lies infinite and often spectacularly beautiful variety. This is less true of the many LEGO® sets we have amassed, which increasingly have come with such detailed instructions that at the end you have a replica of the Millennium Falcon. Little to no imagination required or encouraged.

Thinking about our family play with blocks has helped me to think about what it means for families and family life to be building blocks for society. Families are not static. Families are dynamic; they change and grow (in members, in age, in depth of relationship). They come in all shapes and sizes. I have found it helpful to think less about what a family *is* (what it looks like, what family forms are acceptable) and more about what a family *does*. What do families *do* that make them recognizable as families? They welcome children and other new members. They care for children into adulthood. They care for aging relatives. They feast and fast together. They celebrate and grieve together, work and play together. They forgive again and again.

It may be the case that some family forms are better able to carry out important responsibilities to family members and to society. Taking an example from a global perspective, one could think of the families headed by children in regions of Africa where generations have been wiped out by the HIV/AIDS pandemic. These families struggle in poverty and are less able to pass along important familial, religious, and cultural traditions. A situation in which families are headed by children is not ideal; and the resilience of individual children in the face of such hardship still requires a great deal of support from others. There are also examples where the form of the family, even if it is the "ideal" form (a married male and female raising children), is itself no guarantee against violence and abuse. The ongoing tragedy of domestic violence, especially against women and children, makes this abundantly clear.

Perhaps "family" is more of a verb than it is a noun. What do families need in order to "do the family thing"? What kinds of conditions are necessary for families to raise children, to care for elders and other vulnerable members, to "stay together" even as they may spread out geographically, to pass on important traditions, and to contribute to their communities (from the local to the global)? What do Christian families need in order to act as domestic churches, as schools of solidarity, of love and justice, and as vital participants in the Body of Christ that is the world church? Knowing a bit more about what families need from society and the church puts us in a better position to ask, "What do society and the church need from families?"

The Personal Is Political

One of many slogans of late twentieth-century feminism was "the personal is political." It is an important insight not only for women but for all people and families. Its meaning has two dimensions.

First, "the personal is political" implies that personal, individual choices have political or social implications. What people do influences the world around them for better or worse. There are obvious examples like voting. One's personal action in the voting booth (when combined with the actions of others) determines which candidates and political parties will have greater influence in public policy making and legislation. But other kinds of personal decisions also have a trickle-up-and-out effect as well. For example, decisions that one family makes about how to spend money can fuel a consumer-driven culture on the one hand or create increased demand for affordable, organic produce in their community on the other.

Influence does not flow in one direction, so the second dimension of "the personal is political" is that broader political, social, or economic factors shape personal, family decisions. Parents have the responsibility to protect and promote the health of their children. Certain lifestyle choices that advance the health of children need to be, as Catholic ethicist Lisa Sowle Cahill notes, "real possibilities." A parent can provide a child with nutritious food only if it is readily available and affordable. The same could be said about activities that provide physical exercise. Children can engage in play in the outdoors only if there is safe space to do so. Communities that struggle with high rates of violent crime may find it difficult, even impossible, to secure safe spaces for children. And this is where our two-dimensional look at the relationship between individual families and political, social, and economic structures becomes more complex. The decisions that some families make can either expand or reduce the ability for other families to make healthy choices. Rhetoric that assigns moral praise to families who have many resources at their disposal and moral blame to families who do not fails to capture the complex interplay between personal or familial choices and the social and economic conditions that make those choices possible in the first place.

Families influence and are influenced by the social, economic, political, and faith networks of which they are a part. Within Catholicism, the social teachings of the church address the interaction of these networks and their impact on individuals and communities. Catholic social teaching has been predominately about institutions: about politics and the role of government, and about economics and the role of markets and the meaning of work. Families are impacted by all of these, and families in turn can shape politics and markets through their participation in public life. So it is fitting that an ethic for family life be rooted in these social teachings in a way that could complement, and perhaps refine, perspectives in family ethics that tend to focus on sexual and reproductive issues.

The Plan for This Book

There are any number of excellent books written about marriage and family spirituality and ethics. Many of these have focused on the important issues related to human sexuality and reproduction or on the particular challenges facing families that experience separation, divorce, remarriage, and the blending of families. These are crucial questions for the church and there are many wise and insightful theologians and ethicists who address these complex questions and propose suggestions for pastoral action and public policy.

This text does something different. It takes for granted that families come in all shapes and sizes and will look at family life within the broader contours of themes that recur in Pope Francis's messages about being a church of, with, and for the poor. The media has made much of Francis's commitment to simplicity, his unassuming way of interacting with the crowds of people who come out to see him, and his presence among the poor and vulnerable. While many are experiencing Francis's papacy as something radically new, his statements about the poor and marginalized are deeply rooted in the gospels and the long tradition of Catholic social teaching.

Catholic social teaching has often been called the church's "best kept secret." While many, even those who are not Catholic, know the church's teaching on issues like abortion, birth control, or sex outside of marriage, fewer, even those who *are* Catholic, know what the church teaches about economic systems, the proper role of government in common life, integral human development, immigration, or about the use of force in resolving conflict. It seems that under the leadership of Pope Francis, "the secret is out." He has repeatedly called Catholics, and indeed all people of goodwill, to live joyfully the gospel message that is good news for the poor and vulnerable. This is the lens through which Francis appears to be approaching the many moral issues facing our church and world.

Previous popes and conferences of bishops have written extensively about these themes during the twentieth century. Pope Francis, whose every move is captured by the media, has been a visible and prophetic witness to care for the poor, the vulnerable, and the outcast. To the church's agenda about the pastoral care of families in circumstances including separation, divorce, and remarriage, and the reception of teachings about human sexuality, Pope Francis has added the situation of families living in poverty, families in war-torn regions of the world, and families who are forced to migrate or who are separated by global patterns of migration. Human rights, political instability, violence, globalization, and economic inequality are all "family issues."

The opening chapter, "The Secret Is Out," sets the stage with a brief overview of some of the themes of Catholic social teaching. The core themes that will be reviewed are human dignity, participation in the common good, the option for the poor, and solidarity. It is important to recognize that these themes are not distinct from or independent of one another. Rather, they are related, sharing common resemblances and traits (not unlike a family!), and each theme is always to be understood in light of the others. For example, to be in solidarity with another, one must be committed to one's dignity as a person.

A commitment to the intrinsic dignity of the person provides the foundation for all of the other commitments the church makes. People possess dignity because they have been created by God, in God's image and likeness. People are social and thrive when they are in relationships characterized by love and justice.

People participate in the world around them so that the dignity of all people is respected. The church talks about this participation in terms of "the common good of society." Even as Christians respect *all* people, the Scriptures also call them to a special concern for the poor and vulnerable. Charity is an important way in which Christians answer this call, but it is not the only way. Christians also live in solidarity *with* the poor. That is to say that Christians not only give *to* the poor, they also stand *with* the poor in order to build the more just world envisioned as the kingdom of God.

Solidarity is not a luxury of privileged families. Many of the world's Christians are living in conditions of material poverty. These families have long been standing with and for one another to secure more just living conditions. They have reached out to one another in times of crisis. They give not from their excess (there often isn't any excess); they give from their need like the widow in the Gospel of Luke, who humbly offers a mere two coins at the temple while the rich are boasting about their generosity (Luke 21:1-2). These families are never merely objects of someone else's charity; they are educators in solidarity. Individual Christians first learn about how to live in solidarity in their families, and families in turn can learn how to live in solidarity with one another and perhaps most especially with families who are struggling in a variety of ways.

Chapter 2, "Learning to Live in Solidarity," proposes a vision in which families both resist harmful aspects of our culture and transform that very same culture in order to make the world better for everyone. Families are also essential for the life of the church and have as much to teach as they have to learn about the gospel message of good news for the poor. Families are schools of solidarity, working each and every day to deepen relationships within the family itself and with other families both near and far. Families resist dehumanizing elements of our culture (competitive consumption, wastefulness, violence, etc.) and transform the many arenas of daily life (homes, workplaces, neighborhoods, schools, governments, healthcare institutions, and parishes) so that they honor the dignity of all people, allow full participation in and access to resources, and pay special attention to the poor and vulnerable.

Chapter 3, "*Home*work," looks for opportunities to apply what we have learned about families and Catholic social teaching. It explores the differences that Catholic social teaching and a vision of the family as a school of solidarity can make when it comes to practical decisions in everyday life. If family is a verb, and we know families by what they do, namely by how they live in solidarity within themselves and with one another, then we can ask about the "who, what, when, and where" of family life. How might Catholic social teaching transform our family habits with regard to people, places, things, and time? With whom are we in relationships? Where do we go each day? What do we *need*, what do we *want*, and what do we truly *desire*? How do we use our possessions and the resources of creation? How do we spend our time? How do we mark the seasons of our lives? Do we observe a Sabbath?

This section includes questions for discussion and reflection and suggested activities to build solidarity within and among families. Families can take the time to notice and to celebrate moments of growth and also to notice where we might have our blinders on. Family life is not a competition; we are walking *together* on a long journey. As Pope Francis has noted, sometimes we will find ourselves leading the way, at other times we will be in the thick of the crowd, and there will be moments when we will be taking up the rear, making sure no one is left behind. One step at a time, families can celebrate together when we move in the right direction, and encourage one another when we stumble on the road to solidarity.

The brief concluding chapter, "Say It Joyfully," takes a cue from Pope Francis, who, while he has steadfastly called all Christians to be a church of and for the poor (and this is no easy challenge), has also asked Christians to take up this task joyfully. Families have important work to do, but there is nothing wrong with "whistling while we work"—not to put on rose-colored glasses or a cheery face when times are hard, but to abide in a lasting joy that can sustain us through difficulty. Francis has also called for community of mercy. It is too tempting to be judgmental of other families, often in an attempt to assure ourselves about the moral superiority of choices we have made. It is likewise tempting to see the moral challenge before us as too overwhelming and ourselves as too flawed or limited by circumstance to make any positive and lasting difference. The result is that families either lose themselves on a hamster wheel of activities or they become paralyzed, stuck in habits they would like to change.

In a lecture given to the world's cardinals, Cardinal Walter Kasper noted the vital role that families play in the life of the church and the world:

> [Families need the Church and the Church needs families] in order to be present in the midst of life and in the milieus of modern living. Without domestic churches, the Church is estranged from the concrete reality of life. Only through families can the Church be at home there, where people are at home. Understanding the Church as a domestic church is, therefore, fundamental for the future of the Church and for the new evangelization. Families are the best messengers of the gospel of the family. They are the way of the Church.[1]

Families are not simply waiting to have the good news preached to them. Families are themselves preaching the gospel wherever they go. Through them the church is at home in the world even as families strive to make the world a more hospitable place for all of God's creation. Families need support to "do the family thing," not only from the church but also from other families and every sector of society, so that they in turn can live out their unique vocation to build a world founded on God's justice and love.

1

The Secret Is Out

A Primer on Catholic Social Teaching and Families

Catholic social teaching has often been referred to as the church's "best kept secret" because its teaching on other issues, most notably its teachings on human sexuality, reproduction,

---

"The Lord wants us to belong to a Church that knows how to open her arms and welcome everyone, that is not a house for the few, but a house for everyone, where all can be renewed, transformed, sanctified by his love—the strongest and the weakest sinners, the indifferent, those who feel discouraged or lost."

—*Pope Francis*[1]

---

and abortion (even though they are not always fully understood or accepted) get much more attention from the media and from the pulpit. But the secret is getting out. Perhaps more reserved in his judgments on sexual matters, Pope Francis has nevertheless repeatedly called the church to be a community of the poor and for the poor. He has challenged Christians to go to the "outskirts," the margins of society, to transform the situation for those who are

13

suffering. Pope Francis's prophetic words and actions are drawing increased attention to what the church has to say about suffering in the world, and what the church and other organizations can do about it.

A vague notion about Christian concern for the poor is becoming more concrete as Francis embraces the poor, the outcast, the imprisoned, and those who are ill and disabled. Christians should not think that Francis is talking about "us" and "them." Millions of the world's poor *are* Christian. Christianity is in many ways already a church of the poor who are brothers and sisters in Christ. Francis is making a claim that Christians should be concerned about *all* people who are poor regardless of their religious tradition or culture, and Christians who enjoy some level of power or privilege may have the most to learn from their brothers and sisters who from a situation of poverty are already engaged in the struggle for justice.

"You are the light of the world. A city built on a hill cannot be hid. No one after lighting a lamp puts it under the bushel basket, but on the lampstand, and it gives light to all in the house."

—*Matthew 5:14-15*

Even as the church's commitment to the poor begins to take center stage, many may still be unaware of the key role that families and family life play in Catholic social teaching, not only regarding the procreation and education of children, but also for their participation in building a more just world. While the forms that families take continue to be important to the church, Catholic social teaching tends to focus on what families need so that they can participate fully in society whatever their circumstances. Popes and bishops have written extensively about "the family" and how it is impacted by poverty, violence, discrimination, and unjust working conditions. When the United Nations made declarations about universal human rights and the rights of children, the Vatican contributed (October 1983) a *Charter on the Rights of the Family*. The church has long been an ardent defender of family life, even when people of faith and goodwill have disagreed about the precise conditions that undermine a family's ability to flourish.

It may be helpful to remember in debates about whether the family is in crisis and why that the family does not exist in the abstract. That is to say that there are only *real* families, particular people who have made commitments to one another as spouses, parents, children, grandparents, aunts, uncles, cousins, and so forth. A family's configuration may depend on choice, circumstance, local custom, and legal tradition. It is also helpful to remember that the Catholic Church's view is global in perspective, with an eye toward the universal church throughout the world. The issues that make headlines in the United States, important though they are, may be far removed from the day-to-day concerns of families in the developing world. This global view is crucial and impacts how Christians might think about their responsibilities to families near and far.

This chapter explores the emphasis that Catholic social teaching places on engagement in the world and how it asks individuals and families to "see, judge, and act" in order to bring about a more just and compassionate world. In the process of engaging the world and reflecting on experience in light of the Gospel, the church has distilled several major themes that in turn can guide families in their unique mission in the world: an unwavering commitment to human dignity, the common good of society, and an option for the poor and vulnerable. Taken together these themes provide the foundation for understanding the meaning of solidarity for the church today.

Social Engagement

The introduction to this book discussed images of family life that have gained some prominence particularly, though not exclusively in US culture, including "fortress families" and "havens in a heartless world." While Catholic social teaching has maintained the role that families have in protecting their members, it has also tended to emphasize the relationship that families have *with* and *within* the world. The attitude of Catholic social teaching toward society is characterized more by engagement than it is by isolation. Adopting a more sectarian approach or dropping out of society or the culture at large altogether is neither possible nor desirable for most families.

"The light of faith is unique, because it is capable of illuminating every aspect of human existence."

—*Pope Francis*[2]

For example, some families may seek to insulate themselves from certain aspects of culture or from substandard public schools by home schooling their children. This provides a way to educate children in the context of important values for their family. However, even a choice like home schooling requires certain resources; for example, the family must be able to afford for one parent to be at home with the children throughout much of the day. And even home-schooling parents often need the support of a community of other parents and families to sustain them in this effort. Furthermore, home schooling one's own children does not necessarily absolve a family from contributing to a system that provides education for all children. The challenge is to balance responsibility as parents of particular children with the responsibility that is widely shared for the well-being of *all* children.

While dropping out may be impractical and even undesirable for most families, complete absorption in the culture is no more desirable from a Christian perspective. Christian families may be "at home in the world" but they might often find themselves called to resist certain aspects of the culture around them, whether that is rampant consumerism, competitiveness, or violence. The question is how best to resist those elements of the culture that run contrary to the gospel message of love. Families who cannot grow all of their own food, make their own clothes, earn a livelihood without working outside the home, and meet all of their other needs (which describes most families in the United States) will need to chart a different course.

The emphasis on engagement implies that families of faith are open to the world created by a loving God who looked at creation and called it "good." At the same time they remain alert to its many temptations. In order to live out the gospel, Christian families become involved in work outside the home, in politics, education, healthcare, business, and in other social and cultural activities. For example, in many families, parents have a vocation that is internal to the family: to one another as spouses and as parents of children. They also have other vocations in the world. Though different seasons of family life might mean that one parent focuses primarily on the internal vocation for a time, seasons change. So both parents also have an obligation to minister in the world. It is a juggling act, but this "dual vocation" keeps all members of the family, including children, attuned to the needs of others and allows them to envision their unique participation in the world around them.

See–Judge–Act

The method of Catholic social teaching has been variously called the pastoral circle, the hermeneutical circle (how academics talk about one's lens or vantage point on the world), or the see–judge–act approach to moral decisions. The key to this circle is where it begins; it begins by "seeing," by looking around to observe just what is going on. The process begins with human experience. The Second Vatican Council (a gathering of the world's bishops that met at the Vatican from 1962–65) referred to this fundamental step as reading "the signs of the times and interpreting them in light of the gospel."

In order to begin with experience, Christians take a long look at their own lives and the lives of others. Theologian and noted homilist, Walter Burghardt, SJ, wrote about a spirituality that takes "a long, loving look at the real." Christians need not fear looking at their many blessings and also at times in which they experience hardship, suffering, and pain. They pay attention to the experiences of others, and they *listen* carefully, not necessarily in order to rush in with solutions to problems, but to allow others to have a voice. We might think about the times when we have wanted to share our personal pain with others, not so they could tell us what to do, or how to feel, or to "fix" it for us—we just wanted to be heard as we came to our own interpretations and solutions even though we might need support from others to carry out our decisions.

Moral theologian James Keenan, SJ, has written extensively about mercy as the "heart of Catholicism" and mercy has become a key theme in Pope Francis's papacy. Mercy is often understood in a limited way, as forgiveness. To "have mercy" is to forgive in spite of wrongdoing. Reflecting on the gospel story of the Good Samaritan, Keenan defines mercy as a willingness "to enter the chaos of another." Catholics are called to enter the chaos of people's lives. There is spiritual chaos to be sure, but one might also think about the kinds of chaos that material poverty causes. Jonathan Kozol, advocate for children and teachers, has written powerfully about the chaotic lives of children living in poverty in the United States, particularly about poverty in urban settings that is often combined with racism, crime, high rates of male incarceration, and ill health. This is also the kind of chaos that Christians are called to enter.

In order to respond to the problem of poverty, all Christians must be willing to enter the lives of the poor. They must be attuned to what is going on in the world beyond the front door, beyond the street where they live. Making donations to soup kitchens and homeless shelters is an important element of Christian charity, but visiting the pantry or the shelter to volunteer or simply to be present to those who rely on its services puts a human face on the problem—not just any face. "The poor" is not an abstraction any more than "the family" is. There are particular poor people and families, with unique stories to tell, and listening to their experiences can be transformative; it can change how one sees and understands the problem of poverty that impacts the lives of so many families today.

The second phase of the process involves interpretation or trying to understand what is going on, to make some sound judgments based on experience (but *not* behaving in a judgmental way). To take the experience of poverty to the next step, a sound ethical plan will require an understanding of how people become poor, what keeps them in poverty, and why some communities seem trapped in vicious cycles of poverty, hunger, homelessness, and violence. If Christians want to make a substantial and lasting difference in the lives of poor people, they will need to understand how economies and markets work and how patterns of unemployment and underemployment influence particular communities. They will also need to understand how other factors impact poor people and families, like the impact of racism and/or sexism.

Poverty has root causes, and insight from the social sciences like economics and sociology are vital in formulating responses that will not only be well meaning but effective. Some efforts to assist people in poverty can be well meaning and yet fail to actually help and may even cause greater harm. The "road to hell," as some say, is "paved with good intentions." One notorious example concerned donating powdered infant formula to mothers in developing countries (which may have had more than a purely charitable motive). The communities that received the formula did not have ready access to potable water and so prepared the formula with water that caused life-threatening diarrhea among the infants. A better approach may have been to listen to the experiences of the mothers and involve them in solving an urgent issue regarding the health and well-being of their children. Such engagement might have led to addressing access to water and other nutritious foods for the mothers who could then breastfeed—benefitting the health of mothers and children, indeed entire families and communities.

Charitable responses to poverty are a crucial means by which Christians honor the dignity of the poor in the present moment. Working toward a just society that lifts people out of poverty and provides a way for poor people themselves to participate in building such a society requires legislation, public policy efforts, pastoral programs, and institutional change. A Christian moral response will also include engaging in this kind of critical thinking and working for structural transformation that can be guided in part by insights from natural sciences, technology, engineering, and social sciences like economics, sociology, and psychology.

Christians use information and insight from the sciences, to be sure, but the process of making judgments about a problem also includes theological reflection. Christians read the signs of the times and interpret them "in light of the gospel." So information gleaned through experience and engagement with experts in fields like economics is brought into conversation with the Gospel and the history of reflection on Jesus' message contained in the work of theologians, the lives of the saints, the ritual and sacramental life of the community, and centuries of pastoral practice.

In trying to address the urgent problem of grinding poverty, Christians have a long history to guide them. The "corporal works of mercy" are one instance. In the Gospel of Matthew, Jesus tells a parable in which one group, the "sheep," has fed the hungry, given drink to the thirsty, clothed the naked, welcomed the stranger, and visited the sick and imprisoned. They are the ones who will inherit the kingdom of God (Matt 25:31-36). Throughout the centuries, Christian communities have looked to this parable to inspire concrete acts of charity that address the suffering of people in the here and now.

Kerry Weber, an editor of *America*, a weekly Catholic magazine published by the Jesuits in the United States, has written about her experiences in trying to live out the corporal works of mercy, of entering into the chaos of others who are poor and vulnerable (and insightfully reminding her readers that we bring a little chaos of our own to this endeavor). Her practice of charitable acts like feeding the hungry, giving drink to the thirsty, and visiting the imprisoned was a rich but also unsettling experience that prompted her to ask deeper questions about cycles of poverty and crime and the role that Christians can play in breaking them. The method of Catholic social teaching prompts us then to move beyond charity and toward justice. Those who "have" ought to share with those who "have not." They must also ask why some always seem to have and others have not. What can Christians do to reduce this disparity?

The final phase of the pastoral circle involves a decision and a plan for action. Christians, steeped in the gospel stories about Jesus and his concern for the poor, look among neighbors they know and strangers they don't and see people struggling in poverty. They enter into the chaos of that poverty, perhaps by visiting a soup kitchen or a homeless shelter. They listen to the experiences of particular people. Why are people frequenting the kitchen or the shelter? Research might reveal patterns of underemployment and unemployment after the closing of a factory or mill or the departure of a major corporation in search of cheaper labor elsewhere. If this research highlights the relationship between food insecurity, homelessness, and employment issues, a Christian community might begin a campaign to bring jobs back to the community, lobby representatives to raise the minimum wage, or extend benefits to the long-term unemployed. They might also focus on improving the school programs so that children can envision a future that includes meaningful work that will also earn them a livelihood.

And so the see–judge–act process comes full circle. Christians who engage in this method of moral reflection and action are not simply right back where they started. The pastoral circle may in fact be better understood as a *spiral* in which the long-standing habits of the Christian community—for example, habits of attention to the poor—prompt Christians to seek out certain kinds of experiences and ask certain kinds of questions in the first place. We don't begin the process from "nowhere" but rather as people already shaped by the life, ministry, passion, and resurrection of Jesus Christ. Experiences inspire questions about poverty that are answered in the process of research and theological reflection. Christians act—and through that action they change the situation on the ground and the cycle begins anew.

A Christian community may decide to open a food pantry as the fruit of their experience and reflection. Now that the food pantry is operational, there are new opportunities to be present to those who use its services, new questions to ask about the causes of food insecurity, and a new experience of the gospel message of abundant life and the practice of sharing the eucharistic meal. Further action may spiral the community up toward a greater realization of justice for the poor or spiral deeper and deeper to the root causes of injustice.

In contemplating the life of Mary, Pope Francis has echoed this process of moral reflection and action when he describes Mary's practice of listening, decision, and action. Listening "consists of attention, acceptance, and availability to God." This is no passive or docile practice on Mary's part. She is not merely hearing what is going on. She *listens* to the angel, *accepts* God's will for her to bear a child, and then *goes* in haste to visit her cousin Elizabeth, who is also with child in her old age (Luke 1:26-40). Pope Francis continues, "However, Mary also listens to the events—that is, she interprets the events of her life; she is attentive to reality itself and does not stop on the surface but goes to the depths to grasp its meaning." Her listening leads to decision, "Mary does not let herself be dragged along by events; she does not avoid the effort of making a decision." And decision, the pope says, leads to action, which can be the most challenging part:

> We likewise sometimes stop at listening, at thinking about what we must do; we may even be clear about the decision we have to make, but we do not move on to action. And above all we do not put ourselves at stake by moving toward others "with haste" so as to bring them our help, our understanding, our love—to bring them, as Mary did, the most precious thing we have received, Jesus and his Gospel, with words, and above all with the tangible witness of what we do.[3]

This see–judge–act process of moral reflection and decision within Catholic social teaching is important for families in two ways. First, it is fruitful for individual families who are striving to live the gospel in the world. Families themselves can use this method in order to decide how they can respond to Jesus' call to strive for the kingdom of God. They can use the method to learn more about the experiences of other families so that they can work together for the good of all. They can use the method in their parishes, as a family of families, to discern what kinds of ministries might be most needed in their communities. The "*Home*work" chapter of this book offers suggestions for activities and reflection questions to assist families as they step into this cycle of experience, reflection, and action.

The see–judge–act method is also crucial for families on another level beyond the practices of individual families and parish communities. The church itself—at the diocesan, national, international, and global levels—benefits from adopting this method in its desire to minister most effectively to families. Beginning with a set of teachings and simply applying them to local circumstances in a "top-down" approach may fail to recognize the complex needs of particular families. Through the see–judge–act method that begins at the grassroots or from the "bottom-up," the church could come to a deeper understanding of the challenges facing families today and respond with appropriate pastoral and social justice programs. Pastors, bishops, and cardinals would begin by being present to families and listening—listening to families of all shapes and sizes for the wisdom they hold, listening to other experts and theologians—and allowing what they see and hear in this experience to guide reflection on the gospel message of love and mercy. These experiences in turn would help to shape the church's living traditions, moral teachings, pastoral programs, and social justice ministries.

Through the practice of seeing and listening to lived human experience, interpreting that experience by engaging in thoughtful research, and reflecting on moral issues in light of the gospel, the church has distilled a number of key themes that provide the foundation for assessing ethical action. Catholics do not begin at square one each time they encounter a new problem; there is an accumulated wisdom to guide them. Among the major themes that are touchstones for moral reflection and action are commitments to human dignity, the common good, solidarity, and the option for the poor.

Human Dignity

At the heart of Catholic social teaching is a deep and abiding commitment to the intrinsic dignity of every human person. To say that dignity is *intrinsic* is to say that dignity is not based on any particular characteristic or quality that people possess, such as gender, age, race, ethnicity, economic class, health status, sexual

"God saw everything that he had made, and indeed, it was very good."

—*Genesis 1:31*

orientation, citizenship, and so on. *All* human beings have dignity because they have been created by God in God's image and likeness. Catholics refer to this as the *Imago Dei*, the image of God within us. God gives us dignity, and though we can fail to honor that dignity in ourselves or others, often in some horrifying ways, we cannot give it or take it away in any ultimate sense.

The book of Genesis reads, "Then God said, 'Let us make humankind in *our* image, according to *our* likeness'" (Gen 1:26, italics added). God refers to God's self in the plural. This could have a number of meanings in light of the time and place in which the book of Genesis was constructed. For Catholic Christians, who are monotheistic and believe in *one* god as opposed to many, this notion that God is somehow plural is understood in terms of the Trinity, three persons in one God. A lot of ink has been spilled down through the centuries about just how to understand the Trinity properly, but the take-away point is this: God is relational. God, in Godself, *is* relationship: Father, Son, and Spirit, three persons who create, redeem, and sanctify. If human persons are made in God's image and likeness, then human dignity must also be understood in a relational way.

In the second creation story in Genesis, God says that it is not good for the human creature to be alone (Gen 2:18). Even with all of the gifts of creation about us, we need one another. We are profoundly social, interdependent creatures. That we need one another in order to truly thrive may be obvious, but it is significant and provides an important corrective to many of the messages we hear in a hyper-individualistic culture. We may experience periods of relative independence and dependence, but human beings are always *interdependent*, always in relationships without which we could not thrive. That we need one another is not merely a *fact* of our existence; it is also a profound *good* of our existence. It is good to need each other.

There are times in our lives when we are extremely dependent on others. Infancy is one such season and infirmed, advanced age is another. At other times we may feel more independent, indeed we crave more independence. Any parent of an adolescent knows this from experience; teenagers want to go out on their own, to borrow the keys to the car, to have more privacy, and to make more of their own decisions. And parents of adolescents also often desire that their children take on more responsibility to do things on their own so that they can thrive in adulthood, in spite of the increasing tendency to delay adulthood for as long as possible.

US culture makes much of the desire for independence. It has become part of the very warp and weft of its national story. This culture admires people who succeed by "pulling themselves up by their boot straps" and overcoming whatever odds have been stacked against them (rather than asking why the odds are stacked that way in the first place). People fear losing their independence through aging, illness, or disability and spend considerable sums to remain young and healthy. "Dependence" has become a bad word, as has weakness and vulnerability. No one wants to become a burden on others. We are inspired by people who overcome a tragedy like the Boston Marathon bombing by learning to walk and even run again with prosthetic limbs. We might also think though of the painful conversations that people have with their aging parents about relinquishing car keys, letting someone else do the yard work or cooking, or moving to an assisted living community.

In an individualistic context, dignity, independence, and freedom go hand in hand, but dignity is often talked about in terms of control and autonomy, the ability to choose and decide for oneself. Giving in to vulnerability is a sign that dignity has somehow been lost or diminished. Similarly the concept of freedom can be reduced to the absence of obligations that hinder one's pursuit of happiness.

In the Catholic tradition, freedom is more complex, and indeed may even present a bit of a paradox. The tradition talks about two kinds of freedom: freedom *from* and freedom *for*. Human dignity demands that people be free *from* conditions that undermine that dignity. These include freedom from poverty and hunger, discrimination, persecution, and violence. We might think of President

Franklin D. Roosevelt's "Four Freedoms" speech, given to the US Congress in 1941: "We look forward to a world founded upon four essential human freedoms. The first is freedom of speech and expression—everywhere in the world. The second is freedom of every person to worship God in his own way—everywhere in the world. The third is freedom from want . . . everywhere in the world. The fourth is freedom from fear . . . anywhere in the world."

Famed American artist Norman Rockwell captured these four freedoms in a series of paintings, two of which have families as their subject. In *Freedom from Want*, generations of a family sit down happily to enjoy not just a meager meal but a feast, replete with turkey and trimmings. *Freedom from Fear* depicts parents tucking their two children into bed at night in an atmosphere of warmth and security, even as the father holds a newspaper with headlines about the horrors of war in a distant place. To be free from these assaults on human dignity is crucial to the Catholic vision of human flourishing.

But freedom does not stop there. Freedom from want and fear provides a context in which people can exercise freedom *for* relationships based on love and justice. They are not free from commitments and obligations, but rather are free to take on responsibilities toward intimate others like friends and family, and to more distant others who are in need. This essential freedom is not really about the ability to do whatever one wants, whenever one wants, but a freedom to become a certain kind of person. The paradox is that relationships and responsibilities do not hinder freedom, but allow persons to enjoy a deeper freedom that comes from being in union with others and with God. Even unjust limitations on our freedom, though they must be challenged, do not necessarily eradicate the core freedom persons enjoy as children of God. In the wise words of Nelson Mandela, who in spite of decades of imprisonment under apartheid in South Africa remained truly free, "For to be free is not merely to cast off one's chains, but to live in a way that respects and enhances the freedom of others." This is a crucial insight for families, which might also be said to be schools of freedom for all members of the family. We learn how to exercise our freedom in the context of the family, always holding freedom and commitment together.

Human beings possess an intrinsic dignity that is both profoundly interdependent and free. Yet we know that millions of the world's people are not free from want or fear. They are in relationships, even marital and familial relationships, that are unjust and fail to recognize the intrinsic dignity of all people. This is particularly the case for women and girls globally who are frequently victims of violence and abuse within their own households.

Given that the dignity of human persons and communities is often under assault, the Catholic Church has become an ardent supporter of basic human rights, both economic rights (like food, shelter, housing, and healthcare) and political rights (like freedom of speech, freedom of association, and freedom of religion). Along with its advocacy for human rights, the church wanted to share its wisdom about the profoundly social nature of the person and the family as a building block of society that can make certain claims on the wider community for its protection and support. So in 1983 the Vatican proposed a *Charter on the Rights of the Family*. The *Charter* notes "the family constitutes . . . a community of love and solidarity, which is uniquely suited to teach and transmit cultural, ethical, social, spiritual and religious values, essential for the development and well-being of its own members and of society." Furthermore "the family is the place where different generations come together and help one another to grow in human wisdom and to harmonize the rights of individuals with other demands of social life."[4]

The *Charter* enumerates rights that include the right to marry and found a family; the right to educate one's children in ways consistent with religious and cultural values; the right to social and economic conditions that support their development and their role as participants in the common good of society (a point discussed in the next section). It also outlines rights for families who are immigrants and refugees, families who possess the same dignity as other families and who can make the same claims for protection and support in the communities in which they seek refuge.

Because the church understands the dignity of the person both in terms of the uniqueness of individuals and in terms of our relationships to one another, the church's commitment to human *rights* is always kept in balance with *responsibilities*. Individuals and families have rights and these are the claims that they can make on the community for protection and support. They also have responsibilities to one another and to contributing to the community's ability to offer that support in the first place. Parents may know this intuitively; as children grow and want to have a greater voice in making family decisions, they must also take on greater responsibilities for creating a home in which everyone is supported and heard. Strictly speaking, children do not *earn* the right to be protected and supported, they have that right because they are human, but they do learn to exercise responsibilities that are consistent with their age and ability. So too do all people have responsibilities in their communities according to their circumstances (everyone may not bear identical responsibilities).

Human dignity is at the very heart of Catholic social teaching. All human beings have dignity as persons created in God's image and likeness. Our dignity is fully recognized in our relationships with one another, relationships that begin in the family and extend out toward the community. Our dignity is fully recognized when we are truly free: free *from* injustice and free *for* responsibility and participation in social life. In the ideal, this freedom is first experienced in the family. Our dignity is fully recognized when we are assured certain rights that are both economic and political, and when we are supported in exercising our particular responsibilities. Families also thrive when they are endowed with rights to protection and support on the one hand and full participation in social life and in decisions that impact them on the other. Within Catholic social teaching, it is the tradition of the common good that speaks most energetically about the importance of participation for the well-being of individuals and families.

The Common Good

There is much debate, especially around election time, about the intentions of our "founding fathers" when it comes to the rights of individuals and the responsibilities and the limits of government.

Jane Addams, peace activist and winner of the Nobel Peace prize in 1931, may have had the right idea about our interdependence with one another. Her words would be echoed decades later during the Civil Rights Movement by another winner of the Nobel Peace Prize, Dr. Martin Luther King Jr., "Injustice anywhere is a threat to justice everywhere." We are bound together and the goods of our common life must be widely shared. Furthermore, all people must be able to participate in that common life, in building up the goods that benefit everyone.

"The good we secure for ourselves is precarious and uncertain until it is secured for all of us and incorporated into our common life."

—Jane Addams

To paraphrase the Second Vatican Council, the common good may be defined in this way: the conditions of social living that allow both individuals and communities to readily achieve their flourishing. There are social conditions that keep people from flourishing as individuals, as families, and as larger communities. They include grinding poverty, racism, sexism, political instability, and violence. Conditions that advance the well-being of individuals, families, and communities include economic and political security; racial, ethnic, and gender equality; and peace. It is the responsibility of all people, in light of their particular abilities, to work toward making these conditions a reality for everyone.

Grounded in the gift of human dignity and interdependence, the common good requires that individuals and families pursue goals beyond those that benefit only themselves. As ethicist Thomas Massaro notes, there are many goods that can be achieved only with widespread participation. Some concrete examples of common goods are quality education, public safety, or a sound health-care infrastructure. One form of participation in the common good of education, for example, is paying taxes that go to support schools. Other people participate in making quality education a reality by becoming teachers, administrators, coaches, mentors, and support staff. They take on the challenges and expenses of acquiring the credentials they need in order to teach and work with students. Many parents volunteer their time in schools, assisting teachers, chaperoning trips, and supervising playgrounds. Finally, and ironically often forgotten, is the students' participation. Children are not merely the recipients of what a school has to offer. Children themselves are moral agents who contribute to an atmosphere of respect that creates a space to learn. We all rely on one another for the education of children in our communities.

Because education is a common good it means that it must also be shared. All people have a right to participate in building up a sound public education system, and all people have a right to enjoy the fruits of that participation. Some will benefit because their children are being educated in the schools. People without children, or whose children have grown, or who send their children to private or parochial schools, benefit from having young people educated to be doctors, nurses, lawyers, legislators, business people, public safety officials, ministers, and so forth. Furthermore, *all* children ought to have access to quality schools regardless of the means by which or the degree to which their parents and other adults in their communities are able to participate in building up a school system. On a global scale, all children should have access to a minimum of primary education as a basic human right. Sadly this is not the case, and the lack of primary education has a disproportionate impact on girls that has a ripple effect in terms of women's participation in the common good.

In US culture, which prizes individualism, the concept of the common good is often discredited because it is confused with forms of collectivism or utilitarianism in which the person is valued only insofar as he or she contributes to the group. People have value or dignity because they are useful. The group is more important than the individual, and this creates conditions that easily undermine the dignity of the unique person. But the common good is not utilitarian. The common good maintains the dignity of the person and protects the most vulnerable persons. The common good requires sacrifice, to be sure, but that sacrifice is also shared and never comes at the expense of the dignity of the person. In a situation of injustice, sacrifices are disproportionately shared, with burdens falling most heavily, and repeatedly, on those who are least able to carry them. This is not the common good, but often the exploitation of many for benefit of a relative few who have power and privilege in a society.

Another key concept in Catholic social teaching related to the common good is the principle of *subsidiarity*. It is a bit of a tongue twister, and its root meaning is *assistance*. It is a principle that has often been marshaled to safeguard the rights and autonomy of the family against intrusion by the state. The gist of the concept is this: when problems exist (and they often do) it is best to try to attempt solutions as close to the problem as possible. Society is made up of many different levels of social organization. We have already noted that the family is the smallest, the most basic, building block for all of the other levels and institutions. From families, there are neighborhoods; local and state governments; and national, international and global organizations. The Catholic Church is unique because it exists at all of these levels from the domestic church of the family, to the parish (a family of families), to the diocese, to transnational relief organizations like Catholic Relief Services, and so on, to the Vatican and the global church.

According to the principle of subsidiarity, problems are addressed as locally as possible and larger institutions, like the government, should not interfere or take on responsibilities that are better exercised by smaller institutions like families. For example, as a rule, families are best at raising children. State-run orphanages are not preferable to families. When a family is unable to care for children, another family is sought out (sometimes with the assistance of government agencies). Orphanages are a measure of last resort. Larger institutions like governments offer assistance when necessary, but should not overreach their competence.

Families enjoy a degree of autonomy. Yet families are not immune from interference from other organizations including the state. As an example, it is the proper responsibility of parents to discipline their children and mediate their almost inevitable squabbles. It is the case, however, that in some families the arguments require outside help in order to be meaningfully addressed. Some require the assistance of therapists, and others may even require the intervention of the police and the courts. The painful reality of domestic violence was too long glossed over on the grounds that it is a private family matter. Families are not free to undermine the intrinsic dignity of individual members.

Subsidiarity protects families and local communities from undue interference, but it also requires that other institutions help when necessary. Sometimes local initiatives, to improve a school or playground, for example (which would address important needs of children in the community), will require funding and expertise from others in both the public and the private sector. Parents work with local business people, a town's recreation department, the school board, and maybe with religious congregations, larger philanthropic foundations, and state resources to accomplish this goal. Families and school personnel might design the play space (hopefully with the input of children), businesses and foundations could help fund it, and the local municipality could help maintain it and insure that it meets the requirements for safety and accessibility for children of all abilities. This interdependence creates a space for flourishing; good things happen when people work together. This particular example also might prompt families in suburban neighborhoods to pause and reflect on the tendency to build playgrounds in their backyards for the children in their families. Children whose families have resources need only step outside to find fun, stimulating, and safe places to play where they and their parents may never encounter children who rely on public spaces for recreation.

A Catholic vision of the common good requires participation from all families, and all families in turn, should share in the fruits of what communities can accomplish together. However, Christians pursue the common good for all people with "kingdom eyes" as the Muldoons remind us. Catholics expand the notion of the common good in the here and now to our ultimate common good that is union with God in the kingdom. We might recall the image of the Peaceable Kingdom in the book of the prophet Isaiah:

"The wolf shall live with the lamb,
   the leopard shall lie down with the kid,
the calf and the lion and the fatling together,
   and a little child shall lead them" (11:6).

When the goods of creation and our common life are shared, even natural enemies can live in peace with one another. And there is another surprise: a little child will lead them. While the privileged and the strong surely have a role to play in bringing about the common good, it is the weak and vulnerable who may have the most to teach us about interdependence and God's vision for the world.

Solidarity and the Option for the Poor

From the start of his papacy, Pope Francis has been calling the church to greater solidarity with the poor, who are not objects of our charity but subjects or agents of the new evangelization. The experiences of poor families are the starting point for the church's moral deliberations about how best to live the good news of God's love for us in Jesus Christ. He has asked Christians to listen to what the poor have to teach us about suffering and about liberation. Pope Francis claims "God is not afraid of the outskirts" and neither should Christians be. The outskirts are where Christians meet one another and the poor among us as friends.

Building on the commitment to the intrinsic dignity of all people and working for the common good, the tradition of Catholic social teaching has elaborated this "preferential option for the poor" and a call to solidarity. These are not abstract theological or philosophical concepts, but are rather the fruit of reflection on experience, particularly the experiences of the poor in Latin America who have suffered under colonization, cruel dictatorships and oligarchies (ruled by a few wealthy families), and exploitation by foreign corporations in search of natural resources and cheap labor. The ministers and theologians who worked with the poor in Latin America, listening and looking around, saw Christ crucified again and again in some of the poorest people in the hemisphere. They lived in grinding poverty, toiled at backbreaking work, and lacked any meaningful participation in the governance of their countries. Resistance to these conditions was frequently met with state-sponsored or paramilitary violence.

"The word *solidarity* is a little worn and at times poorly understood, but it refers to something more than a few sporadic acts of generosity. It presumes the creation of a new mind-set that thinks in terms of community and the priority of the life of all over the appropriation of goods by a few."

—*Pope Francis*[5]

There were instances in which the institutional church failed to speak up on behalf of the poor and helped to maintain the status quo. This did not stop people from gathering to break open the word of the Scriptures and to break bread together in the Eucharist. The God they encountered there—in the story of the Exodus from Egypt, in the words of the prophets calling for justice, in the proclamation of the kingdom by Jesus who came to bring liberty to captives and good news for the poor—was a God of justice and liberation, a God who hears the cries of the poor and acts decisively on their behalf.

If God in Jesus Christ has made an "option for the poor," that is to say to stand with the poor in their suffering, then this is what Christians are called to do as well. The measure of any personal or family decision, pastoral plan, public policy, or economic theory is how it will impact the lives of the poor who have the most urgent claim on our resources of time, treasure, and talent. Choices that primarily benefit those who have power or privilege at the expense of the poor are immoral. They fail to meet the demands of the gospel. This solidarity means that Christians will listen and look around and will work *with* the poor, who are often already giving from what little they have by way of material goods to support one another and are already engaged in the struggle for justice.

This may also mean that Christians will forever find themselves on the outskirts challenging the status quo—it is not often a popular place to be.

Physician Paul Farmer, who has dedicated his life's work to the destitute poor of Haiti (and through the organization Partners in Health to the destitute poor all over the world), speaks about "the O for the P," his shorthand for the option for the poor and what it will cost those who make this option with their lives: "How about if I say, I have fought for *my whole life* a long defeat?" He continues, "You know, people from our background . . . we're used to being on a victory team, and actually what we're really trying to do in [Partners in Health] is make common cause with the *losers*. Those are two very different things. We *want* to be on the winning team, but at the *risk* of turning our back on the losers, no, it's not worth it. So you fight the long defeat."[6]

Farmer's insight into solidarity and the option for the poor is important. When Christians strive to work for justice, to make a real change in the world, they may experience victories along the way, but they will also have to face loss and will need courage so as not to give up hope. Solidarity needs to be steadfast in a world that tempts us to success that often comes at a price paid by the poor. Saint Pope John Paul II wrote of solidarity: "This then is not a feeling of vague compassion or shallow distress at the misfortunes of so many people, both near and far. On the contrary, it is a firm and persevering determination to commit oneself to the common good; that is to say to the good of all and of each individual, because we are all really responsible for all."[7]

Watching the evening news is enough to move people to "vague compassion" and "shallow distress" until we change the channel to something more comforting. Concern for others living in poverty or amidst violence and persecution remains superficial because making an option for the poor asks so much of us.

Because making an option for the poor is so challenging, solidarity may be best thought of as a virtue. Virtues are habits that we acquire through practice. They don't come naturally but by trying again and again, even if we fail on our first attempt. It is a lot like exercise: we try a new regimen slowly at first so that we test, but don't injure, our muscles. We might start out with a walk around the neighborhood and once we do that with relative ease, we work our way up to a jog. We go farther and farther as our stamina increases. Our time improves. We might join a club or run with a friend. We try the 3K, the 5K, and the 10K, and some enter a marathon. Friends, family, even strangers, cheer us on at the finish. If we really want to transform a sedentary life and run a marathon, we don't start by running 26.2 miles! That is a road to injury and the chance that we might return to the couch and the remote control. Solidarity, the "long defeat" described by Farmer, is not a sprint, but rather a marathon and it requires training and a community of support if we are to stay in the race.

"This is why I want a Church that is poor and for the poor. They have much to teach us. Not only do they share the *sensus fidei*, but in their difficulties they know the suffering of Christ. We need to let ourselves be evangelized by them. The new evangelization is an invitation to acknowledge the saving power at work in their lives and to put them at the center of the Church's pilgrim way."

—*Pope Francis*[8]

Charity, as people say, begins at home, but doesn't end there—likewise, solidarity. With young children, a family might remember the poor at prayer before meals or contribute to Catholic Relief Services' Operation Rice Bowl during Lent. Families might gather up outgrown clothes for donation to the Saint Vincent de Paul Society or take a tag from the parish "giving tree" during Advent. They learn about people in need, and they learn that they have a role to play in helping them.

With these habits established as children grow, new possibilities can be tried. Families can work in the food pantry or the soup kitchen, deepening their relationship with the poor. They might go together to a Habitat for Humanity site or help tutor children in a nearby shelter. They might lobby for homeless families at their state house or stand with members of Pax Christi to oppose capital punishment or violent conflict. Families that give from what they have might begin to make more sacrifices, to change how they view success, to live without things they had previously taken for granted. They can recognize the ways in which many of the advantages they enjoy are linked to the suffering of others (like affordable food and clothing, or technological devices that require much fought-over natural resources).

Slowly, but surely, the option for the poor and solidarity can become second nature. Members of a family that first learned to care for one another, learn then to care for others, especially the poor. They learn that *their* participation in the struggle for justice is necessary and they are ready to run the marathon, together. Christians learn habits of solidarity in the family so that they may befriend families who are suffering. Families learn to see, judge, and act. This engagement with the world around them provides families with insight about the dignity of all people, about what is needed to build the common good, and how they can stand in solidarity with the poor and vulnerable. Families are sustained in these habits by the church, a "family of families."

Families are schools of solidarity—or training grounds. It is in the family that we learn to flex our muscles. Parents try to set an agenda for the growth of the family, seeking out experiences that will be challenging but not overwhelming. As in any other kind of school we begin with our ABC's, not with *War and Peace*. Members of a family first learn that they are loved, then to care about one another, neighbors, strangers, and even enemies, especially those who are poor and suffering. Members of a family also learn that the family itself is a kind of common good—where everyone is loved and respected, where everyone must pitch in, and where everyone can enjoy the home they have "built" together.

2

Learning to Live in Solidarity
A Practical Spirituality for Families

The tradition of Catholic social teaching is rich, and though the preceding chapter offered only a glimpse of its method and major themes, there is a lot to absorb. So it is time for a pause, a study hall in our school of solidarity, to review what has been covered so far and what it might mean for family life, and to imagine what might lie ahead.

How do families *learn* to live in solidarity with other families and with all who are poor and vulnerable? How do they resist destructive aspects of the culture around them? How do they engage that very same culture in order to transform the world, making it a more just and compassionate place for all people? What do families have to *teach* the church about what they have learned?

Families build special bonds within the family, bonds of love and fidelity. These bonds are deeply personal and support each family member as a unique individual created and loved by God. But in spite of being personal and welcoming of unique individuals, family life is not absolutely private or individualistic. Families are not only defined by the personal and intimate relationships between spouses, parents and children, siblings, and others. Families are also social and public—they turn outward toward the common good. Families themselves are communities of life and love but they also participate in many other communities as well:

"In the family, everything that enables us to grow, to mature, and to live is given to each of us. We cannot grow up by ourselves, we cannot journey on our own, in isolation; rather, we journey and grow in a community, in a family."

—Pope Francis[1]

neighborhoods, schools, churches, workplaces, and volunteer organizations. Indeed, it may be said that without this participation on the part of families, society itself would suffer, and the ties that hold communities together would weaken considerably.

To be a school of solidarity, a family must be willing to look at what is going on in the world. As noted in the previous chapter, the Second Vatican Council called this "reading the signs of the times." One theologian has called it taking "a long, loving look at the real." These two phrases are packed with meaning, but there are two key points to be made in thinking about families and solidarity.

The first point is that *Catholic families are interested in what is going on in the world and engaging with others*, with a particular focus on the many ways in which people are suffering today. Families are interested in trying to address that suffering by devoting some of their resources to charitable giving and by supporting ministries that help people in the urgency of the present moment by feeding the hungry, giving shelter to the homeless, or visiting the sick and imprisoned. As families flex their solidarity muscles, they take the risk of leaving the haven of the home to encounter in a personal way those who are poor. As Pope Francis has made clear, the poor have much to teach us, and those who enjoy some privilege in society have much to learn, not just as students of the poor, but also as friends. And the stronger we become in living in solidarity the more likely we will be not only go to the "outskirts" but also to transform our homes into havens of another sort, where those who are weary and suffering find welcome.

Catholic families are also interested in understanding what is causing suffering at its roots. The "signs of the times" are not merely individual events in history but also encompass trends. Why are so many individuals and families without a place to call home? Why are many parents unable to provide nutritious meals to their children? Why are families, particularly in some urban communities, dealing with the incarceration of so many men and boys? Why are some people facing illness alone, and why are so many others struggling to care for both young children and elders without respite? Why are so many communities shaken by violence and scarred by racism and multiple forms of discrimination? Why are girls among the poorest of the poor across the globe? Why is the air unfit to breathe and the water unfit to drink?

The answers to these "why" questions are vexingly complex and require serious and careful thought as well as prayerful reflection. As complicated as the underlying factors may be, some clear patterns are likely to emerge: patterns of unemployment fueled by an uninhibited desire for profitably among corporations; discrimination based on race, class and gender; the stigma of illness and disability; a "throw away" culture of waste that is devastating the environment.

Understanding these root causes of injustice and the ways in which they are often linked to one another (for example, poor communities are often disproportionately impacted by pollution that in turn causes ill health) helps to determine the kinds of actions that might improve the lives of those who are suffering and paves a way to support others in their struggle for a better world. Just as patterns of injustice emerge when people think carefully about the world's problems, so too do patterns of wisdom emerge from theological reflection and centuries of pastoral commitment to the poor and vulnerable. Respect for the dignity of all people, a commitment to the common good that we can only build together, the special claim that the poor have on us, and the call to live in solidarity with others are the refrains heard over and over again. They become the touchstones for family life.

The second point is that looking at what is going on in the world is a *look of love*. There are times when looking at another with love seems to come easily: looking at your future spouse as you approach the altar for the sacrament of marriage; looking into the barely opened eyes of a newborn baby; looking at children when they play together merrily; looking at the joy on a child's face when you have volunteered in a community center or mentoring program. At other times, looking lovingly is a bit more challenging: looking at your spouse after a bitter argument; looking at that same newborn after a night (or several nights) without sleep; looking at our children when they fight over a toy or act disrespectfully toward others; looking at a homeless person who is filthy and inebriated.

So the love we are talking about is more than a warm, fuzzy feeling that makes your stomach do flips or gives you a jolt of positive energy. This love, Christian love, is grounded in the firm belief that we are loved by God. It is a steadfast love that helps us not turn away when the sights are unpleasant or when the relationships we are trying to build and sustain have drained us. In words attributed to St. Camillus de Lellis, a sixteenth-century priest who dedicated his life to the care of the sick: "Commitment is doing what you said you would do, after the feeling you said it in has passed." This is the kind of steadfast, *solidaristic* love we are talking about. It is a love that keeps us in the game and moving together toward a goal in the confidence that the good feelings, which are not at all unimportant, will return by God's grace. Caring for others and working for justice is challenging for individuals and families, and Catholic social teaching presents many arduous tasks to be sure. But our relationships are not merely burdens to be born with resignation. They are also gifts in which we find delight and glimpse God's gracious love for us.

Christians are called to live in solidarity, to live with and for others, to look lovingly at reality, and from that love strive to make the world more compassionate and just. Christian families are also called to this solidarity *as families*. The tradition of Catholic social thought has made an insightful claim: families are "schools of solidarity." This takes the call to solidarity a step further. What does schooling in solidarity look like? Part of the answer seems obvious: parents educate their children. They pass on important values, traditions, and practices. They tell the Christian story and strive to live out that story with practices of prayer, worship, service, and work for justice. Parents seek out experiences for their children to grow in compassion and in the ability to ask questions and pursue answers. Many of these experiences begin in the home by caring for siblings and elders and taking on increasing responsibility for the tasks of the household (cleaning, preparing food, welcoming company, etc.). Parents strive to know when and how to stretch the family's muscles, opening spaces for the kind of tension that brings about creative growth.

"Tell me and I forget, teach me and I may remember, involve me and I learn."

—*Benjamin Franklin*

A staple of Catholic teaching is that parents are the primary educators of their children. But this is not a static, one-directional mode of education. As the above insight from Benjamin Franklin makes clear, people learn best when they are involved in the task at hand. The participation of *all* members of the family is necessary, and the task of children is not limited to merely obeying and imitating their parents. To honor the dignity of children, a family that lives in solidarity will welcome the very unique contributions of children. For example, it may be simple to say that parents teach their children to be patient by practicing waiting in a variety of contexts: waiting in line at the grocery store (boring!), sitting through Mass (which unfortunately can also be boring!), waiting in line at the amusement park (so hard, but the reward so tantalizing!), and hardest yet, waiting weeks and months for a birthday or Christmas present.

But it is also true to say that parents learn much about patience from their experiences with children: slowing and bending down as toddlers learn to walk; stretching an hour-long car trip to two or three hours with pit stops for potty training; sitting beside a child for hours as he or she struggles with a new math concept or sounds out the words of a favorite story; letting young people learn by doing even when it would be faster and easier just to do it yourself; adopting new habits and routines to benefit a child with special needs. And adults in the family may need to learn patience anew as an elder parent ages, slows down, or becomes forgetful and confused. We are all always learning from one another about how to live and how to love. Schools are dynamic places. My personal experience as a teacher has shown me that our classrooms are better and richer for the very unique students who gather together to become part of a learning community. I can always learn something new about a subject I have been teaching for ages. So too can families learn something new about the meaning of the Christian story from one another.

In the school of solidarity there are no rigidly defined roles of teacher and student even though parents and other adults assume special responsibilities for children and vulnerable family members. The lesson plan may be crafted by parents who have a sense of what their children need to learn to grow, but there are many days when the plan goes out the window in the face of unanticipated questions, confusions, and experiences. Yet the class does move forward, and important goals are reached even if the journey takes several detours. And sometimes what seems like an interruption is actually a graced opportunity to care well for one another. The gospel calls us all to grow and to keep growing throughout our lives as disciples.

Another reason that it is helpful to think about the family as a school of solidarity is that schools benefit their communities. The closing of schools is disruptive to communities not merely because it creates an inconvenience for parents and children who must adjust to a new school; its loss is felt by everyone who sees the school as an anchor or as a zone of protected space for young people in a neighborhood. What is learned in the family is not merely for the advantage of the family; it is also for the benefit of others who are neighbors and strangers. Families are able to deepen the bonds of fidelity to one another but are also able to build bridges to other families. Unlike other kinds of schools, there is no graduation date; learning about solidarity is a lifelong endeavor, and as families grow and change over time, new opportunities to discover the meaning of solidarity present themselves.

These family networks and the "family of families" in a parish are able to provide the support that individuals and families need to make difficult choices about how to resist aspects of the culture that undermine human dignity and relationships and how to transform the world around them. Families might change their patterns of consumption by buying less, recycling, supporting businesses with a track record of treating employees with dignity, reducing their impact on the environment, or eating differently (and maybe less) based on health and environmental impact. These choices often mean walking past most stores at the mall and products in the grocery aisle. They may mean spending more on fewer things if you have the resources to do so. It may involve a change of career if this is possible (many of us must "bloom where we are planted") or passing up a promotion that would take more time away from family life but might have funded the trip to Disney that the children are pining for. It is important to note that these decisions, when they are real possibilities for families, will involve being countercultural. Parents and children both may struggle with the sacrifice of not wearing the latest fashion, not having the latest technological gadget, not having the prestige that comes with some forms of success, or not getting a fast-food treat on a busy day. It's good to have company if you are swimming upstream. Families can be that company for each other so that resistance does not become isolation.

Families who are in a position to *give up* any number of things that our society tells us will make us young, happy, and secure may find that they then have more to *give to* the world around them. They may find more time and energy for participation in parish life and other civic and social organizations, more resources to support important causes about which they are passionate, or a deeper sense of living their vocations in the home and in the world. Resistance does not lead to isolation but to engagement and transformation.

Families are schools of solidarity in which everyone has a part to play, sometimes as teacher, sometimes as student. Family members learn from one another. They learn through experience. They learn through study, prayer, and participation. They learn from

the stories of the Scriptures and from the lives of saints gone before. They learn *from* and *with* the church as the Body of Christ
alive in the world today, made up of rich and poor and everyone
in between. Yet, while families are doing all of this *learning* as
families, what may be forgotten or ignored are the ways in which
families can *teach* the church, enriching its wisdom about human
dignity, the common good, the option for the poor, and solidarity.

If the church wants to learn more about the intrinsic dignity
of the person, it can look to family practices. Too often this view
gets short-circuited when the church, more as teacher and less as
student, thinks only about marriage and reproduction, ensuring
the dignity of the person even in the very earliest stages of human
life. This is an important message, but there is more to dignity than
this. Families welcome children, to be sure. They welcome children
for who they are and who they grow to be. One theologian has
noted that, even though many parents might not think this way
at first, the act of becoming a parent is the most extreme act of
welcoming the stranger as one created in God's own image and
likeness. Many parents (and indeed many of the relatives looking
on) think first about the child being the "image" of one's father,
or mother, or aunt, etc. We think about how children are "like us."

But before long, families experience this new member as someone absolutely unique and discover more and more about the ones
they love. Perhaps families who grow though adoption know this
best of all. We don't know yet what the children's gifts and talents
will be, but we trust they are there. We don't know yet what their
unique challenges will be, but we'll face them together. We don't
know with what or with whom they will fall in love, but we know
that welcoming children will lead to welcoming others into our
homes and our lives.

Families cannot know at the outset how their members will
grow, change, and age. We cannot know what will be asked of us
in sickness and in health, in good times and in bad. This is risky
business. As Pope Francis has said, "We are afraid of God's surprises. Dear brothers and sisters, we are afraid of God's surprises!
He always surprises us! The Lord is like that."[2] If the church wants
to live more deeply its commitment to human dignity it can learn

from families how to welcome everyone and how to find yet another place at the table to which we bring our offerings as well as our hunger. The church might just find itself surprised, maybe even "surprised by joy" at the family that has gathered.

The church learns from families about dignity and solidarity not because families are perfect, but perhaps precisely because they are not. Pope Francis has called the church a "field hospital" for sinners, and Cardinal Kasper has extended this image to families "where it is necessary to bind many wounds, dry many tears, and establish reconciliation and peace time and again."[3] Many parents never knew how good they would need to be at peace building! Families may grow in fidelity and solidarity but they are not immune from hurt. Family squabbles, misunderstandings, and betrayals can have profound and lasting consequences. Letting go of an old grudge takes tremendous effort, and moving toward reconciliation requires an abundance of God's grace. But many families find the strength to do just that, to mend what has been broken or torn and stitch together a union that is even stronger than before. That is not to say that reconciliation and peace building necessarily keep a family or a marriage together. Sometimes that is not possible as a way forward.

Even in these moments of brokenness, and perhaps especially in these moments, the church can learn from families about how to walk with one another through pain and about how changing relationships are not necessarily a sign of weakness but may in fact be a sign of courage. It is in these moments that the church community can make an option for the poor and vulnerable, by listening to the voices of families who are struggling for whatever reason. If the family is a common good, built by many hands for the good of all, then the church too can become a common good to which every family, no matter how wounded or broken, contributes and from which every family draws strength and grace.

Now we know the players: families of all shapes and sizes who are striving to do "the family thing" by growing in solidarity. We know what motivates them: the life and ministry of Jesus and his proclamation of the kingdom of God. We know where many of the challenges lie: in deeply rooted habits of injustice in our societies and in the temptation to build fortress families that are disengaged from the world. We know what families need: all kinds of support to carry out their unique mission in the church and the world. And we know the major themes that can guide a practical spirituality of family solidarity: human dignity, participation in the common good, and the option for the poor. Where can the story go from here? How might family schools of solidarity transform their relationships with people, places, things, and time—the stuff of everyday family life?

3

Homework

Hands-on Learning, Field Trips, and Recess

When I teach courses in moral theology to college students, I try to convey key moments in the church's history, the major themes that lay the foundations for the church's teachings and the urgent moral questions facing the church today. This is all well and good, but eventually we come to the "so what?" question. Students want to know what any of this has to do with them and their lives. I find myself asking similar questions no matter how many times I might teach the same course: "What does all of this really mean? How would I, my family, my community, and my church be living if we really believed in human dignity, the common good, and the option for the poor? What does solidarity, which looks so good on paper, look like in practice?" I am reminded of conversations I have with students who major in the sciences for whom the chemistry or physics lectures may be interesting, but for whom the excitement really begins in the lab, where they get to test the theories and actually *do* something hands on.

In the laboratory of everyday life, families are constantly navigating among various relationships and responsibilities to family, neighborhood, community, workplace, parish, and so on. Christian families do this as they strive to live as disciples of Jesus who came preaching the kingdom of God and good news for the poor and vulnerable. Some of the opportunities and challenges that discipleship and a commitment to solidarity bring for families have been introduced in previous chapters; now we can look at these possibilities in a more practical, hands-on way.

The world's problems are many and they are complicated. To consider your family's role in meeting the world's needs can be a daunting task, one that can lead to cynicism or a sense of hopelessness about what can be achieved. This feeling that the problem is too big can leave us feeling paralyzed, afraid to move, or feeling that we can't make any meaningful difference in the way the world works. Or it may keep us constantly engaged in a flurry of activity

---

"Yesterday is gone. Tomorrow has not yet come. We have only today. Let us begin."

—*Blessed Teresa of Calcutta*

---

without taking the time to think about what we are doing and why. The authors of a guide to social action called *The Better World Handbook: Small Changes That Make a Big Difference* (see "For Further Study" at the end of the book) note that people need to avoid the trap of despair and opt instead to enter a cycle of hope. Among their suggestions are envisioning a better world, becoming informed about the world's problems, taking action, and finally "recognizing that you can't do everything." Their words echo a prayer attributed to Archbishop Oscar Romero, who was martyred in El Salvador in 1980 (though these words were never actually said by him): "It helps, now and then, to step back and take a long view. . . . We cannot do everything, and there is a sense of liberation in realizing that. This enables us to do something, and to do it very well. It may be incomplete, but it is a beginning, a step along the way, an opportunity for the Lord's grace to enter and do the rest." Along similar lines, wisdom from Saint Francis of Assisi suggests that we begin with what is possible in the here and now, aware of both our gifts and our limitations. If we make a beginning, however modest, the cycle of hope begins and a space opens for grace to enter, making more things possible all the time.

"Start by doing what's necessary; then do
what's possible; and suddenly you are doing the
impossible."

—*St. Francis of Assisi*

Christians today live in a "don't just stand there, do something!"
culture. It is crucial that we take action when we see others who
are suffering or when we encounter an injustice. This may mean
leaving our comfort zones and taking a "field trip" to encounter
the lives of others whom we may not meet in our daily lives. We
go to the outskirts of our lives and communities. And yet Christian
families don't just keep themselves busy, measuring success only
by what we accomplish. Christian families are "contemplatives
in action." Christian families also say, "Don't just do something,
stand there!" Christian families are called to reflect on the world,
to really listen with care to the voices of people around them and
not only rush in with frenetic activity.

Christians are called to be daydreamers in the best sense of
the word. Having a vision of what the world could be, of how
it could be more like the kingdom of God, also requires a lot of
imagination. And imagination requires time and space to grow—a
recess of sorts. Parents of young children often see imagination at
play when children take whatever they have at hand to transform
an ordinary room or yard into a place of wonder and adventure.
Sadly, this sense of imaginative play can be lost as we grow and
our sense of what is possible begins to narrow with the weight of
responsibility and being practical. Swimming against the tide of
a cynical culture that limits the possible (and accepts the status
quo, the ways things are, as inevitable) will require that families as
schools of solidarity reclaim time and space for daydreaming and
play. This is not *wasted* time, but rather time that can open families
to new experiences and possibilities. In one sense, when Catholic
Christians gather at mass, we are imagining what the world could
be like if people came together, reflected both on a shared story and
their uniqueness before God, exchanged a peaceful embrace, and

broke bread around a table at which there is room for everyone and plenty to go around. We imagine abundant life for all, and we pledge to take what we have imagined and try to make it a reality.

The following sections look at family life through the lens of Catholic social teaching and its commitment to human dignity, the common good, the option for the poor, and solidarity. We will explore relationships to *people, places, things,* and *time.* Each section incorporates a series of discussion and reflection questions along with some activities that help families think more deeply about their role as schools of solidarity within the church. These questions and activities can encourage practices that suit your family's needs in the present moment and also provide a creative space to think about how your family may be called to greater solidarity and imagine the possibilities for living out that call.

"It always seems impossible until it is done."

—*Nelson Mandela*

The questions and activities engage the method of Catholic social teaching: beginning with experience (both the experiences in our families and stretching out to encounter experiences of those on the outskirts), then engaging in reflection on those experiences, and moving toward actions that are both charitable and just. The order is not meant to be rigid; families should feel free to move around throughout the sections as the Spirit moves them. Since the method of Catholic social teaching involves seeing and listening, and analyzing and reflecting, before making a decision, the actions and activities suggested here are less about making big sweeping changes and more about gaining some new experiences.

The goal is to provide a guide for learning, reflecting, dreaming, and making sound ethical judgments about the gifts and tasks of family life. The intent is not to be judgmental, finding that your family is not quite up to snuff. Neither is it a "to do" list to be checked off in order to feel better about our families and move on. It is an invitation that families can come back to again and again as circumstances change.

Encourage *every* member of your family to participate according to each person's age and ability. Allow every member of your family to be heard. Hopefully, the questions will help families uncover the values that are truly important to them and what they most deeply desire for and from one another. Take what you find helpful and leave the rest, keeping in mind that some questions and activities might be challenging or uncomfortable and yet at the same time may provide a growing edge for your family. Remember that this is about lifelong growth—so stretch your family's solidarity muscles as you are able. As some habits develop, try something new. Some of the activities that are challenging might also be fun.

Set out on this journey remembering Pope Francis's call to mercy and be gentle with yourselves and with each another. Together take one step at a time. Also recall Francis's invitation to a life of joy that comes with knowing we are loved by one another and by God.

People: Relationships, Rights, and Responsibilities

During my childhood *Mr. Rogers' Neighborhood* was a staple of children's television programming aired on public broadcasting (PBS) channels. Fred Rogers was a Presbyterian pastor who maintained close friendships with both Catholic priest and spiritual writer Henri Nouwen and Jonathan Kozel, a tireless advocate for children. Mr. Rogers is remembered, however, for his kind and gentle spirit. Viewers watched as he entered his stage home and traded his jacket for a sweater and his walking shoes for a pair of sneakers while singing "Won't You Be My Neighbor?" Rogers wanted young people to get to know the world and the people around them without fear and in a context of security and trust. He wanted children, so often asked to be seen and not heard, to know that their feelings and their voices matter. He knew how important everyone is to a community, including children. He knew that everyone has a role to play in making a neighborhood just that, a community of people that cares for and about one another. He also knew how people could hurt one another. One thing that was remarkable about Fred Rogers was the way he took children seriously and spoke to them with respect. His example demonstrated what it meant to honor the dignity of children who are vulnerable and depend on adults for care but who are also capable of contributing to their families and communities.

> "Then the Lord said to Cain, 'Where is your brother Abel?' He said, 'I do not know; am I my brother's keeper?'"
>
> —*Genesis 4:9*

What is true of children is true of all of us. All people experience vulnerability and the need to rely on many kinds of relationships for their well-being. All people have something to contribute to those crucial relationships. All people should be treated with respect and compassion. This is what it means to take human dignity seriously. Families know that they have special responsibilities to the members of their family, especially to members who are particularly vulnerable, whether they are children, elders, or members facing illness or disability. They know that we have been given into each other's care.

Families whose lives are shaped by the gospel also know that they have responsibilities to neighbors and strangers. They know that they are members of a family united by baptism and that all people are members of the human family. So they navigate these many relationships of faithfulness and justice, ever widening their circles of solidarity. They ask themselves questions about how their choices and actions impact the lives of the poor both near and far. Families with limited access to resources nevertheless give generously from what they have.

This is no easy task, and all families need support. Many families need support in accessing food, clothing, shelter, healthcare, and education. Many families need networks that sustain them in meeting particular family responsibilities. We might think about networks that support families who have children with disabilities or networks that offer respite to families caring for elders with dementia. Many families need support as they make challenging

"'Teacher, which commandment in the law is the greatest?' He said to him, 'You shall love the Lord your God with all your heart, and with all your soul, and with all your mind.' This is the greatest and first commandment. And the second is like it: 'You shall love your neighbor as yourself.'"

—*Matthew 22:36-39*

decisions about how they will use the resources they have, keeping love of God and love of neighbor at the center of their lives. They will need support as they stand up for the rights of all people and families. No family can do this alone.

Families who want to grow in solidarity by recognizing the dignity of all people might consider the following questions and activities about the relationships they have with family members and others, especially the poor and vulnerable.

People You Know

- Who are the people in your lives? Make a list beginning with your immediate family and move outward. Encourage all the members of your family to add to the list. Each member of your immediate family is unique, yet part of the same body. What particular gifts and challenges do the members of your family bring to your family life?

- Many families have Christmas card lists. Who is on yours and why? There is a trend in sending pictures of children and pets, scenes from vacations, and Christmas letters detailing the activities of the year gone by. Do you enjoy or feel pressured by this activity? Why or why not? Are there people in your life that you contact only at this time of year?

- What practical steps do you take to maintain relationships with friends? What do you enjoy about your friends and friendships?

- Are most of your friends like you (in age, gender, racial identity, family financial status, interests)? Are some of your friends different? What do you appreciate about or learn from those differences?

- Do you know your children's friends or the friends of your parents or siblings? What do your children or parents like about their friends? What do you like about them?

People to Get to Know

- Shortly after the debut of *Mr. Rogers' Neighborhood*, the Children's Television Workshop launched *Sesame Street*, which asked children "Who are the people in your neighborhood?" Do you know the people in your neighborhood or apartment building? Do you know other families in your parish?

- Are the people in your neighborhood or social circle alike in terms of race or class? What are the barriers that keep your family from getting to know families whose backgrounds are different from yours? Can you think of ways to address these obstacles?

- Are there some people you "see" most days who also remain "invisible": people who clean your office, church, or school? People behind the fast food window or at the coffee shop counter? People checking out groceries and other purchases? Delivering your mail? Driving school buses, trains, taxi cabs? Were these people on the first list you made about people in your life? How do you and your family usually interact with some of these people in your life? Do you look past them? Perhaps you could try saying "hello" and introducing yourself to someone you encounter frequently but don't really know. How might knowing someone's name and calling that person by name change your relationship?

- What about those people who are truly hidden from view? People who harvest your food or make your clothes? How can you make these people more visible to your family?

Ministry Opportunities

- What ministries does your parish offer specifically for families?

- Think about the ways in which many ministries impact family life: a food pantry ministry, visits to those living in nursing homes, the parish school, or a religious education program. How can these be opportunities for families to minister together as families rather than being segregated by age (youth groups, activities for retired persons, etc.)?

- Technology can be very helpful in learning about the lives of families far away, particularly about families who are struggling in poverty, political instability, and/or violence. Take a look at websites like Jesuit Refugee Services and Catholic Relief Services (the links are listed in "For Further Study"). What steps can you take to be in solidarity with these families?

- What charitable activities could your family engage in (donating money, clothing, food, etc.)?

- In what ways could you accompany poor families in your community? Is there a local food pantry or shelter? Is there a nursing home? Could your family visit the elderly there, especially those whose families live far away and are unable to visit regularly? This is a way of caring not only for people in the nursing home but for their families as well.

- What activities could you engage in to better understand and help change the conditions that have impoverished some families? Examples to explore include: talking to the coordinators of social service agencies about what they have experienced and learned about the root causes of poverty; writing to your local and state representatives to Congress and the Senate about the struggles facing people in your community or about your concern for families across the globe; writing a letter to the editor of your local paper; writing to your local bishop to share your experiences of service and solidarity; educating yourself about how various public policies and laws impact the poor—you can visit websites including the United States Conference of Catholic Bishops' "Forming Consciences for Faithful Citizenship" or Catholic Relief Services (both found in the "For Further Study" section).

Places: Here, There, and Everywhere (Even Cyberspace!)

Families "do the family thing" in lots of different places including their homes, neighborhoods, schools, workplaces, places of worship, and even in the car! Learning to live in solidarity with other families necessarily involves getting out and about; the school of solidarity takes field trips. Schools of solidarity cherish their time at home but also find their home in the world. Christian families can make Christ present in all the places that they visit, and they can also encounter Christ in some unexpected places. Thinking about places to visit also prompts us to think about what we hope to find and about the people we might meet. Reflecting on the many places in which our families do their thing might also lead us to consider how to make the world a better place for all families.

Your Place at Home

- Do you think about your home as a safe haven or a fortress? What do you find reassuring about these images? What do you find limiting?

- Is your home like a school? In what way?

- Is your home a beehive of activity? If so, what do you like about that?

- How would you describe your home, neighborhood, town, or city using your five senses (sight, sound, touch, smell, taste)? Perhaps your family could take a tour of your town or city, not merely driving through on the way to somewhere else, but rather to pause and use your senses.

- In what way does your home provide a place of rest?

- Is your home a place of hospitality? Who visits your home? Are there opportunities to welcome strangers and make them friends? Perhaps your family could make a plan to invite another family to your home just to get to know one another better.

"I long, as does every human being, to be at home wherever I find myself."

—*Maya Angelou*

Places Away from Home

- What places do you visit in any given week or month? Work? School? Commercial businesses and stores? Churches? Athletic venues? Entertainment or cultural sites (movies, museums, libraries)? How much time do you spend in the car? In nature? What kinds of feelings do you experience in these spaces? Try keeping a journal or a list of the places you visit. What patterns do you see?

- Do the places you visit welcome all people? Do poor families have access to these places? Why or why not? Do people with disabilities have easy access? What things could your family do to make more people feel welcome?

- Where do your travels take you? What places do you dream about visiting? What do you find attractive about these places? Whom do you meet there?

- In what places and spaces do you find comfort? Are their places you find especially beautiful? Are there places you find threatening or ugly? Why?

- What places do you think of as sacred or holy? Are there places where you experience God's loving presence? Places where you can pray? Churches might be one example but there could be many others. Places in nature? A beach by the ocean? A crowded city street? Places in your home? The dinner table? A favorite chair?

Ministry opportunities

- Do you ever visit places outside of your comfort zone? Pope Francis has called Catholics not to be afraid of going to the outskirts, to the margins of society (keeping in mind that the outskirts may not be far away and may even be in the center of a city or town). Where would you like to go and why? Do you face challenges to this practice, especially if there are small children in your family? Once you have tried this, what did you learn?

- What can you and your family do so all families have access to the kinds of spaces that help them thrive?

- Are there opportunities to visit or work with family shelters, women's and children's shelters, neighborhood playgrounds, care centers for children and elders? What action can you take to make sure that there are adequate school and play environments for all children?

- What can you do to provide space for play and imagination (for children and adults!) in your home? At work? In your parish?

Cyber Places

- How much time does your family spend in cyberspace? Does time on computers, tablets, and smartphones enhance your existing relationships or help you to build new relationships? Does your family feel able to leave the online world and be present to one another in the place that you find yourselves (at home or in the car, for example)?

- If you surf the net, what websites do you visit? What and whom do you find there? Do you shop online rather than in stores?

- Try a "tech fast" for a day (or fasting from technology that is not required for your work or education). Or keep a "tech use" journal. What do you use technologies (computers, smartphones, social networking, tv/dvd/dvr, video games) for? What needs and desires does your use of technology meet? Can you think of other ways to fulfill those desires?

- Have a conversation about what you like about technology, video gaming, virtual reality, and social networking. What don't you like? Do you feel pressured by others' use of technology? What rules about technology use and social media do you think are reasonable and helpful and why?

- Can you think of ways to use technology in order keep abreast of social justice issues that are important to you and your family? Can you use technology to visit other parts of the world to see how other families live?

Things: Needs, Wants, and a Culture of Consumption

In the eighties, stand-up comedian George Carlin did an entire routine on stuff. "Your house is a pile of stuff with a top on it. You gotta lock it up, while you go out and get more stuff!" People laughed at Carlin and at themselves. It was funny because it was true. Many of us have a lot of stuff. If you have small children you probably have even more stuff—strollers, highchairs, pacifiers, sippy cups in every color of the rainbow, toys, toys, and more toys . . . stuff that you bring with you wherever you go . . . just in case. We buy homes and vehicles that can hold all of our stuff. We are often weighed down by our stuff.

We often don't know who makes our stuff anymore. Where did that cell phone come from anyway? Where did the parts come from? Who made my sweater or my shoes? It also seems to be the case that they don't make stuff like they used to. Our stuff breaks or becomes obsolete in the blink of an eye. No one knows how to fix or mend stuff anymore. So we toss it out or turn it in for the newest model knowing that it is only a matter of time before we'll need another new one. And even if some of our stuff lasts, it goes out of style so we regularly need new clothes, new handbags, new cars, new kitchens, etc. All of these become status symbols by which we measure our own and others' worth. We befriend those who are like us, those who dress in similar ways, drive similar cars, take similar vacations—and all the while a competitive spirit with respect to consumption is working below the surface (and sometimes not so far below!). As a society, we are no longer trying to keep up with the Joneses; we are trying to outdo them.

This is the "culture of waste" spoken about by Pope Francis. He notes that this cultural phenomenon "tends to become a common mentality that infects everyone." Even families with few resources are often caught in a never-ending, work-to-spend cycle that has consequences in high rates of exorbitant debt and a near constant

---

"Jesus answered, 'If you wish to be perfect, go, sell your possessions, and give the money to the poor, and you will have treasure in heaven; then come; follow me.' When the young man heard this word, he went away grieving, for he had many possessions."

—*Matthew 19:21-22*

---

feeling that one never has enough, or "if only" I had that phone, car, video game or whatever, I could be happy. The big business of advertising is shaping our desires to sell us something on the one hand and always leaving us somehow unfulfilled on the other.

Francis goes even further in his assessment of what is happening in a world where more is always better. According to Francis, "whenever food is thrown out, it is as if it were stolen from the table of the poor, from the hungry! I ask everyone to reflect on the problem of loss and waste of food, to identify ways and approaches that, by seriously dealing with this problem, convey solidarity and sharing with the underprivileged."[1] The pope claims that the more people accumulate and waste is directly related to the lack of basic needs among the poor. Having too much and tossing it aside is tantamount to stealing.

The culture of waste fueled by consumerism is essentially a disposable culture as well. We see the impact on the environment as landfills brim with items that seep into the earth and the water supply. It also has effects on people, and those effects are not limited to debt and the ill health caused by pollution. A culture that views things as disposable is in danger of thinking of some people as disposable as well. In our race to consume more and more, there are lives that are consumed, wasted, working in inhuman conditions for pitiable wages so that goods will be more affordable elsewhere. Cheaper clothes can result in a closet overflowing with clothes that we may never even wear. To use Francis's analogy, the clothes I have unworn in my closet have been taken off the backs of the poor. This is a far cry from "I was hungry and you gave me food . . . naked and you gave me clothing" (Matt 25:36).

A discussion about our relationship to things quickly brings us back to our relationships with people. Some of our relationships with people might be shaped by our patterns of consumption and competition. People are drawn together less by common interests or commitments and more by what they have. And our patterns of consumption create unjust relationships with those whose lives may remain largely hidden from view but who are inextricably linked to us in the supply and demand chain. How I feed and clothe my family impacts the ability of other parents to feed and clothe theirs. Our need for stuff brings us into a web of relationships with others for whom we share some responsibility.

That is the dark side of stuff. And it should be resisted by families who measure themselves by how well they live in solidarity with the poor. It should be resisted by families who believe that no one is disposable. But that is not all that can be said about stuff. It may be too simplistic to say that Christians "put people before things." People need things. Human beings are consumers. We need food to survive—we do not make our own energy. We need clothing and shelter that are appropriate for the climate in which we live—we don't carry shells on our backs. We need to get from here to there, and our circumstances may involve getting somewhere that is too far away for walking. We need access to medicine and other technologies when we are ill.

Human dignity demands that these basic needs be met. Human dignity also demands more than mere subsistence. It is a good thing when we have access to education, books to read, music, art, and culture that lift the human spirit. And all people should be able to access these things. That is why schools, libraries, and museums are in a sense "common goods." We are not merely consumers with basic needs for survival; we also *desire*. There are strands within the traditions of Christianity that talk about desire as if it were a bad thing, leading us down a road of temptations that must be resisted. This may be true when our desires are directed toward those things that can never really satisfy our deepest longings. Our very deepest desires as Christians, when we take the time to discover them, are to be companions of Christ, to be in union with God and one another, and to experience peace and joy.

So having stuff is not the problem. People need stuff. Part of the problem may be that some have too much stuff while others don't have enough. We often fail to see the connections between our consumption of stuff and the impact that this has on the poor. Another part of the problem may lie in not being able to distinguish our basic needs and our deepest desires from our more fleeting wants. That we have desires is not the problem; that we settle for what television advertisements say we should desire is. Pursuing these desires will only fuel restless consumerism and the irony is that we are stuffed and empty at the same time.

What then is a school of solidarity to do?

Needs and Wants

- Take a look around at your stuff. What do you have? Do you have what you need to care for your family? Do you have enough? Too much?

- A group called New American Dream, which is trying to confront consumer culture, uses a slogan "more fun, less stuff." They asked people to take a picture of all of their shoes and post the photos to the organization's website. How many pairs does your family own? What feelings are sparked in you when you look at the pile?

- As a family make a list of your needs and of your wants. Are there items you have trouble categorizing? (In our house, for example, everyone seems to *need* a phone and not just *any* phone, but a smartphone.) Have some things you once thought of as luxuries become necessities? Why?

- To think about the things you value, play "the desert island" game. If you were stranded, what three things would you want with you and why?

Culture of consumption

- Pope Francis has talked about a "culture of waste" that is becoming pervasive in society. It is devastating to our environment and is degrading to persons who also become "disposable." Try a journaling activity: keep track of what your family wastes (thrown away food and packaging). Do you see any patterns? Buying too many groceries? Discarding usable objects in favor of something newer or more fashionable? Are there missed opportunities to "reduce, reuse, and recycle"?

- Have each member of your family choose one clothing item that you could try to trace to its roots or find out more about the store that sold it to you or the company and the workers that made it. Be prepared, this is no easy task!

- Though there are many reasons to curb our habits of consumption, shopping is often a necessity. Very few of us grow all of our own food, make our own clothes, and so forth. How can families use their purchasing power to make the world a better place? Take a look at guides like *The Better World Shopping Guide* by Ellis Jones (see "For Further Study") to review what kinds of practical changes might be possible for your family.

- Not all Christians are called to vows of poverty, and God's plan is that we all have life and have it abundantly. It is not the case that families need to eke out only subsistence living. It is possible and perhaps desirable for most of us to enjoy some "luxury" that lifts the human spirit. Eighteenth-century German writer Goethe (author of *Faust*) once said, "A man should hear a little music, read a little poetry, and see a fine picture every day of his life, in order that worldly cares may not obliterate the sense of the beautiful which God has implanted in the human soul." Though our moral language often casts culture as something to be resisted, what elements of culture (books, movies, works of art, etc.) draw you and your family deeper into human experience and the experience of the sacred? They do not necessarily need to be explicitly religious in content. What are some of your favorites?

- My husband and I confess to not liking all of our children's music, as generations of parents have before us. But the music does speak to our children about how they are feeling on the rocky road of adolescence and about their dreams for the future. Try a day or a car ride with "headphones off" so that your family can share playlists—even if it is painful at first!

- What are your habits of feasting and fasting? What do you enjoy about these experiences? What do you find challenging? Are their ways to simplify some of your celebrations?

- Could your family devote some resources to a worthy cause? Maybe give up something for a short while (or maybe a long while) so that your family could make a donation to an organization that you choose together? Perhaps your family could give up eating out or going to the movies if your family does these things frequently. Visit Charity Navigator for helpful ideas about organizations and information about how they allot their resources (http://www.charitynavigator.org).

Time: Seasons and Sabbath

For the last ten years, my family, together with my parents, my sisters, their spouses and children, has gone on a summer vacation to Cape Cod, Massachusetts. It is a fun week of swimming, sand castles, kites, and lots and lots of ice cream. My children are among the older of the cousins, and it has become possible for my husband and me to actually read a book, have a conversation, or sip lemonade while keeping an eye on them. My youngest sister has an eighteen-month-old son. On his first trip to the Cape at the age of seven months, he stayed wherever he was put. At eighteen months, he was running everywhere, desperate to keep up with the older ones, and absolutely loving the pool. As my sister and her husband chased after him, another sister said, "Welcome to the working vacation!" We were all trying to find a time for family, for rest and rejuvenation, a time free from work and other responsibilities, but the seasons of our lives were also different. We needed to come together as a family of aunts, uncles, cousins, and grandparents to make that kind of time possible by watching over little ones so parents could go out, take a swim, or a nap!

"The Sabbath is supposed to be a day of being available for God, and also a day of being available for feasting and celebrating together, a day of leisure with and for each other (see Exodus 20:8-10; Deuteronomy 5:12-14)."

—*Cardinal Walter Kasper*[2]

Journalist Brigid Schulte recently wrote a book called *Overwhelmed: Work, Love, and Play When No One Has the Time* (New York: Sarah Crichton Books, 2014). People feel pressed for time, feeling as if they have less time for what really matters to them. Boundaries of time and space are more porous: we bring work home (children have long been doing this even before the age of the home computer); we shop from home in the middle of the night; we may bring our children to work. This has certain advantages in terms of convenience and does alert us to the reality that our lives do not fit into neat little compartments that never touch each other. However, multitasking has become a prized virtue in our culture, always doing more than one thing at a time: driving while talking on the phone, doing the Christmas shopping on a laptop while making dinner, checking email at a child's soccer game. There is growing evidence to suggest that while we think we excel at multitasking, especially by using technology, we actually can't do two things at once, or at least we can't do either of them very well. We can't be truly present to the task or the person before us.

So thinking about time, like thinking about places and things, also brings us back to thinking about people and relationships. We think not only about how we spend our time but also with whom. How do we find time to give others our full attention so that the bonds between us can grow and flourish? How do we devote time for activities that we value that might include meaningful work but also prayer, recreation, hobbies, and conversation? Do the ways in which we spend our time benefit others, especially the poor?

Christians mark time in a number of important ways. They observe the Sabbath (which is something increasingly difficult to do when we are pressed for time) because God has made time holy. Resting on the "seventh day" is important for Christians because the Scriptures tell us that God rested on that day having created the world and called it good. So we too have a day of rest. We

---

"A generation goes, and a generation comes, but the earth remains forever."

—*Ecclesiastes 1:4*

---

are reminded in the Exodus story of Moses and the deliverance of the Israelites from their captivity in Egypt that the people of God are no longer slaves, and we observe a day of rest and worship to remember what God has done for us. We observe a Sabbath gathering for worship at the Eucharist to strengthen our vision and our commitment to insuring that no one is a slave—no one is held captive by fear, poverty, discrimination or violence. Our sacred time has a social dimension. It strengthens the bonds of solidarity in our families, our parishes, and with those who seek justice in the world.

Time is holy and not just on the Sabbath. Christians also mark time during the liturgical year. We have seasons of anticipation and longing like Advent, seasons of repentance like Lent, and seasons of hope and joy like Christmas and Easter. We observe holy days that recall moments in the life of Christ, the church, and the lives of the saints. Christians develop special practices to suit the time: lighting an Advent wreath, fasting during Lent, or exchanging gifts at Christmas. And then we have "ordinary time" all those other days that are no less sacred for their ordinariness. Ordinary time, like ordinary life, is holy, and spending time in prayer and attentiveness can open Christian families to the many graced moments in our day-to-day lives. Time passes throughout the year and the cycle begins anew.

How do schools of solidarity spend their time in the service of human dignity, the common good, and the option for the poor?

Family Time

- What does your family calendar look like? Where and how do you spend your time? What does your calendar reveal to you about your priorities and your values? Like the "tech use" journal, try keeping a time journal for a day or a week. What opportunities did you discover to change how you spend your time?

- Are members of your family overwhelmed by activities and work? What strategies might you employ to reclaim time for what is most important ? Perhaps trying to eat together more often or turning off electronic devices like cell phones.

- How would you define leisure time? Does your family play together? Does your family get enough rest?

- More and more families designate time as family night or date night in order to protect some time for their relationships. Does your family do this? Has it helped strengthen your relationships? Is this a practice that your family could try? What are the potential downsides to designating special times for relationships (rather than making time everyday to be with one another)?

- Is some of your time spent in service to others outside of your family, especially the poor and vulnerable? Does your family perform service together?

- Think about the "seasons" of your family's life: seasons during a year (for example, the "new year" for you might be "back to school" in late August) or over the course of many years. Are you caring for very small children, teenagers, or elders? Does work take you outside the home? Are you entering a new phase: starting a new job, retiring, beginning a family with children, or preparing for an empty nest? How do you prepare for or celebrate a change of season?

- What seasons during the year do you find especially joyful? What is your favorite season (either in a religious sense or simply the time of year, like autumn)? Why?

- Are there seasons that you find especially stressful? Why? For example, Christmas is a time of great joy for the Christian community as we celebrate the incarnation, God becoming human in the person of Jesus Christ and sharing in all of our joys and sorrows. Yet many people find this among the most stressful times of the year as the pressure to prepare an ideal holiday weighs heavily (and we begin shopping before Columbus Day to insure this). Many people experience loneliness or disappointment when all of the gift giving is over.

- Have there been seasons of illness or disability? Unemployment or financial insecurity? What have these experiences taught you and your family about time?

- Does your work allow you to take vacation time? Do you use it?

- Does your work allow you be away on weekends or some days during the week on a regular basis?

- Is there time in your family to rest from housework? Who in your family comes home from work outside the home to cook, clean, do laundry, help with children, or care for elders? Is this work shared in your household or does one member do most of this?

"For everything there is a season, and a time for every matter under heaven."

—*Ecclesiastes 3:1*

Sabbath Time

- Who are the people you see working on the weekends, especially on Sundays?

- Think about people in your community and in the world who do not have a day of rest but who must work every day (often at more than one job) to make ends meet. Say a special prayer for them on your day of rest. Learn more about working conditions in the world for adults and for children by visiting the website of the International Labor Organization at http://www.ilo.org/global/lang--en/index .htm.

- Do you observe a Sabbath? What does Sabbath mean to you? Rest from work? Attending church services? Time for fun? What are the challenges you face in this practice?

- Are you and your family able to carve out regular sacred time and space? For prayer together or alone?

- Does your family spend time together? Do members of your family enjoy time alone? When and where is this possible? What are the obstacles you face? Are there forms of support that you wish you had to make this a reality? Do you need help from family, friends, or coworkers? Are there ways you could support members of your family or other families?

- Plan ahead for a Sabbath day together as a family. Decide how important work and daily tasks will be accomplished so that the whole family can enjoy a day of rest and prayer. What kinds of activities will you allow and what will you avoid? Watching television, video games, reading, listening to music, cooking, playing, hobbies? Will you take the day off from youth sports that often take place on Sundays? Do you think you would have support in doing this or meet resistance? Do members of your family agree on what a day of rest looks like?

• Plan as a family for how you could observe one of the liturgical seasons of the year like Advent or Lent. How could some of your choices impact the lives of those who are poor and suffering? If you give up something for Lent, could you donate the money you might save through this practice to your favorite charity? Could you provide Christmas gifts or a celebratory meal to a family in need? Could you make a plan to limit your spending during the Christmas season or spend time and resources in ways that focus on relationships instead of things?

Schools of solidarity are open to challenging questions, to deep reflection on important ideas and values, and to engaging in activities that stretch the mind, body, and soul. Hopefully this list has prompted you and your family to ask, answer, and act in ways that strengthen relationships within your family and with others. Perhaps you have generated even more questions and imagined new possibilities for your relationships with people, places, things, and time. It may be only a beginning, but it is "a step along the way, an opportunity for the Lord's grace to enter and do the rest."

4

Say It Joyfully
A Progress Report

There are families of all shapes and sizes living out the gospel message of love in their everyday lives. This is to be celebrated. They are doing the family thing with two parents and sometimes with one, with young children and without, with access to important resources and privileges, and from situations of poverty and vulnerability. Some of these situations arise by choice and some by circumstance. Children are being cared for and raised into adulthood. Elders are being honored as they face aging, illness, and disability. Spouses are supporting one another in good times and in bad. Friends, neighbors, and even strangers are welcomed into homes. Families are joining together with other families to build communities where people flourish.

"I have said these things to you so that my joy may be in you, and that your joy may be complete. 'This is my commandment, that you love one another as I have loved you.'"

—*John 15:11-12*

Pope Francis has noted that families are places in which "*unity and diversity* know how to merge in order to become a great source of wealth."[1] Families are unique and they are united; they are not *uniform*. Our diversity, like our interdependence with one another, is not something to be feared or regretted, but rather is a source of richness. It is the way of solidarity and not an obstacle to it. In this way the fabric of family life can be a model for our churches.

"Keep the joy of loving God in your heart and share this joy with all you meet especially your family."

—*Blessed Teresa of Calcutta*

As schools of solidarity, families are places where each unique individual is welcomed and loved for who he or she is. All family members, at one time or another, act as teacher or as learner. Some learn from others who have more experience and wisdom. Others learn through the questions and vulnerabilities they encounter or when someone asks "why?" over and over again. Our churches too can recognize that all members of the church, as individuals and as families, have something to teach and something to learn as part of the community.

As schools of solidarity, families look out onto the world and see the goodness of God's creation and also the shadows cast by human sinfulness and suffering. Their look is one of love and not one of condemnation. This look of love is practiced in the home as families face their own weaknesses and the hurt that somehow only loved ones can inflict on each other. Families must practice peace building each and every day. Many families act to bring peace to communities made more vulnerable by violent crime. They stand as parents, grandparents, aunts, uncles, siblings, and cousins against violence, fear, and hatred. Solidarity brings families together to move toward reconciliation. The wisdom and experiences of families can be lessons for the church as parishes strive to seek forgiveness from those who have been estranged and offer welcome to all even in the wake of pain, disappointment, and the loss of trust.

As schools of solidarity with no graduation date, a family's work is never done, and the fruits of being a family—much of the good that comes from being a family—lies in the future. As the Romero prayer puts it, "This is what we are about. We plant the seeds that one day will grow. We water seeds already planted, knowing that they hold future promise. We lay foundations that will need further development. We provide yeast that produces far beyond our capabilities . . . We are prophets of a future not our own." The good that families do lives on in future generations, so families can live in hope. Families who stood together in solidarity during the Civil Rights movement in the United State knew this very well. They fought for rights that would not be realized in their lifetime, but fought instead for their children and their children's children. These families kept a vision alive, not as just wishful thinking, but as a deep commitment that required tremendous sacrifice, and that to this day requires solidarity across race and class and every other line that divides our communities.

"But we must also say and say it joyfully: there exist very good families, which do their best to live the faith of the church and give witness to the beauty and joy of faith lived in the bosom of the family. They are often a minority, but they are a distinctive minority."

—*Cardinal Walter Kasper*[2]

If we were to tell our children that they are in school "for life," this might not be met with shouts of joy. They often eagerly await Friday afternoon from the moment the first bell rings on Monday morning. We can't blame them. School is hard. It asks a lot of us. There may be as many setbacks as there are successes. There are people with whom forming friendships seems easy, and others with whom it is difficult to get along. School can be a place of learning, dreaming, and building relationships only if everyone takes responsibility, students and teachers alike. If everyone pitches in and everyone is respected, then everyone benefits.

This lifelong learning is what Catholic social teaching asks of families, and in turn, lifelong learning is what families ask of the church. Families need to be supported in concrete ways in order to exercise their responsibilities at home, in the world, and in the church. They need to be honored for the wisdom they bring about human dignity, building the common good, and making an option for the poor and vulnerable. As schools of solidarity, families will indeed be able to live joyfully even as they make sacrifices for one another and the church, the "family of families" in Christ, will rejoice and be glad.

Notes

Introduction

1. Cardinal Walter Kasper, *The Gospel of the Family* (Mahwah, NJ: Paulist Press, 2014), 25.

Chapter 1

1. Pope Francis, "A House That Welcomes All," General Audience (October 2, 2013).

2. Francis, *Lumen fidei* (encyclical letter on the light of faith, June 29, 2013), 4, 34. Online at www.vatican.va.

3. Francis, "Her Example," address at the end of the Marian month of May (May 31, 2013).

4. Charter on the Rights of the Family, Preamble E, F. Online at www.vatican.va.

5. Francis, *Evangelii gaudium* (encyclical letter on the joy of the gospel, November 24, 2013), 188. Online at www.vatican.va.

6. Qtd. in Tracy Kidder, *Mountains beyond Mountains: The Quest of Dr. Paul Farmer, A Man Who Would Cure the World* (New York: Random House, 2004), 288.

7. John Paul II, *Sollicitudo rei socialis* (encyclical letter on the thirtieth anniversary of *Populorum progressio,* December 30, 1987), 38. Online at www.vatican.va.

8. Francis, *Evangelii gaudium,* 198.

Chapter 2

1. Francis, "A House of Harmony," General Audience (October 9, 2013).

2. Francis, "The Christian Message," homily for the Easter Vigil (March 30, 2013).

3. Cardinal Walter Kasper, *The Gospel of the Family* (Mahwah, NJ: Paulist Press, 2014), 14.

Chapter 3

1. Francis, "The Cult of the God of Money," General Audience (June 5, 2013).

2. Kaspar, *The Gospel of the Family*, 9.

Chapter 4

1. Francis, "A House of Harmony," General Audience (October 9, 2013).

2. Kaspar, *The Gospel of the Family*, 2.

For Further Study

For use at home

Muldoon, Tim, and Sue Muldoon. *Six Sacred Rules for Families: A Spirituality for the Home.* Notre Dame, IN: Ave Maria Press, 2013.

For use in the parish or classroom about Catholic social teaching

Himes, Kenneth R. *101 Questions & Answers on Catholic Social Teaching.* 2nd ed. Mahwah, NJ: Paulist Press, 2013.

Hudock, Barry. *Faith Meets World: The Gift and Challenge of Catholic Social Teaching.* Liguori, MO: Liguori Publications, 2013.

Massaro, Thomas. *Living Justice: Catholic Social Teaching in Action.* 2nd classroom ed. Lanham, MD: Rowman & Littlefield, 2011.

For in-depth reading on Catholic social teaching

Dorr, Donal. *Option for the Poor and for the Earth: Catholic Social Teaching.* Maryknoll, NY: Orbis Books, 2012.

Himes, Kenneth, ed. *Modern Catholic Social Teaching: Commentaries and Interpretations.* Washington, DC: Georgetown University Press, 2005.

For material on virtues and the practice of mercy

Francis, Pope. *The Church of Mercy.* Chicago: Loyola Press, 2014.

Kasper, Walter. *Mercy: The Essence of the Gospel and the Key to Christian Life.* Mahwah, NJ: Paulist Press, 2014.

Keenan, James F. *Moral Wisdom: Lessons and Texts from the Catholic Tradition.* Lanham, MO: Rowman & Littlefield, 2010.

Keenan, James F. *Virtues for Ordinary Christians.* Lanham, MO: Sheed & Ward, 1996.

Keenan, James F. *The Works of Mercy: The Heart of Catholicism*. 2nd ed. Lanham, MO: Rowman & Littlefield, 2007.

Weber, Kerry. *Mercy in the City: How to Feed the Hungry, Give Drink to the Thirsty, Visit the Imprisoned, and Keep Your Day Job*. Chicago: Loyola Press, 2014.

Vatican documents on the family

John Paul II, Pope. *Familiaris Consortio* (Apostolic Exhortation on the Role of the Christian Family in the Modern World, November 22, 1981).

Paul VI, Pope. *Humanae Vitae* (Encyclical Letter on Birth Control; July 25, 1968).

Charter of the Rights of the Family (October 22, 1983)

These are available online at the Vatican website (http://w2.vatican.va /content/vatican/en.html) along with materials from the Extraordinary Synod on the Family called by Pope Francis for 2014 and 2015. Cardinal Walter Kasper prepared a reflection on family life for the synod called *The Gospel of the Family* (see full citation below).

Catholic moral theologians writing on marriage and family life

Bourg, Florence Caffrey. *Where Two or Three are Gathered: Christian Families as Domestic Churches*. Notre Dame, IN: University of Notre Dame, 2004.

Cahill, Lisa Sowle. *Family: A Christian Social Perspective*. Minneapolis: Fortress Press, 2000.

Kasper, Walter. *The Gospel of the Family*. Mahwah, NJ: Paulist Press, 2014.

Lawler, Michael G. *Marriage and the Catholic Church: Disputed Questions*. Collegeville, MN: Liturgical Press, 2002.

McCarthy, David Matzko. *Sex and Love in the Home*. Norwich, UK: SCM Press, 2004.

Ravizza, Bridget Burke, and Julie Donovan Massey. *Project Holiness: Marriage as a Workshop for Everyday Saints*. Collegeville, MN: Liturgical Press, 2015.

Rubio, Julie Hanlon. *Family Ethics: Practices for Christians*. Washington, DC: Georgetown University Press, 2010.

Resources on resisting consumer culture

Beaudoin, Tom. *Consuming Faith: Integrating Who We Are with What We Buy.* 2nd ed. Lanham, MO: Sheed & Ward, 2006.

Jones, Ellis. *The Better World Shopping Guide: Every Dollar Makes a Difference.* 4th ed. Gabriola, BC, Canada: New Society Publishers, 2012.

Jones, Ellis, Ross Haenfler, and Brett Johnson. *The Better World Handbook: Small Changes That Make a Big Difference.* Gabriola, BC, Canada: New Society Publishers, 2007.

Websites on Catholic social teaching in action

Catholic Relief Services, http://www.crs.org

"Forming Consciences for Faithful Citizenship (USCCB)," http://www.usccb.org/issues-and-action/faithful-citizenship

Jesuit Refugee Services, http://en.jrs.net/index and https://www.jrsusa.org

Network: A National Catholic Social Justice Lobby, http://www.networklobby.org

United States Conference of Catholic Bishops, http://www.usccb.org

Websites for resisting consumerism

The Center for a New American Dream, http://www.newdream.org

Common Sense Media, https://www.commonsensemedia.org

Websites about world poverty and the plight of families across the globe

Caritas Internationalis, www.caritas.org

Catholic Relief Services, http://www.crs.org

Jesuit Refugee Services, http://en.jrs.net/index and https://www.jrsusa.org

UNICEF (United Nations International Children's Emergency Fund), http://www.unicef.org

United Nations Millennium Development Goals, http://www.un.org/millenniumgoals